40 EXERCISES FOR A BETTER BUTT

The Ultimate Workout Book for Great Glutes and a Perfect Posterior

JASON CURTIS

FUNDAMENTAL LIFESTYLE

40 Exercises for a Better Butt

The Ultimate Workout Book for Great Glutes and a Perfect Posterior

Published by **www.fundamental-lifestyle.com**

ISBN: 978-1-78933-023-6

www.fundamental-lifestyle.com

Cover Image Copyright: Shutterstock 4 PM production

For more information about the author:

Website: **www.5sfitness.co.uk**

Facebook: **www.facebook.com/5sfitnessuk**

Instagram: **www.instagram.com/5s_fitness**

Twitter: **www.twitter.com/5sfitness**

YouTube: **http://bit.ly/2GksRK1**

Other Books from Fundamental Lifestyle

Fix Your Posture:
The Simple Exercise Solution

Free Yourself from Aches and Pains Caused by Bad Posture

• Discover simple, yet life-changing posture correcting exercises and techniques.

• Understand how to fix your seated, standing and sleeping posture and reduce aches and pains.

• Build healthy posture habits that will have you living pain free.

20 Essential Exercises for Bigger Biceps:
Quickly Build Big Biceps with Targeted Weightlifting Programs

Build big biceps in 20 easy exercises

• Learn how to build strength and muscle mass

• Develop healthy weight training habits

• Master workout programs to supercharge your gains

Strength and Mobility Exercises for Runners

Improve your Running Speed, Mobility and Strength

• Simple, effective exercises and example programs to follow

• Understand how to build strength, speed and mobility to become a better runner

• Build healthy training habits that will drastically improve and lengthen your running career

15 Essential Exercises for Bigger Triceps:
Quickly Build Big Triceps with Targeted Weightlifting Programs

Build big triceps in 15 easy exercises

• 15 effective exercises and example programs to follow

• Safe training programs to reduce the risk of injury

• Complete, easy to follow breakdown of every tricep-building exercise

The Gym Journal: A Workout Log Book
The Ultimate Fitness Journal to Track Your Training and Achieve Your Exercise Goals

Includes professional advice from top UK coach on:

• Programming training for maximum benefit

• Effective warm-ups

• Strength and resistance training

This comprehensive training diary will help you track any kind of training.

The Daily Food Nutrition Journal:
A Log Book & Food Diary to Track Your Eating Habits

Not just another log book / food diary...

• Accurately track and record your nutritional intake

• Discover your weaknesses: are you eating too much or too little?

• Monitor your long and short term goals

Contents

Introduction

This book details 40 exercises that will not only develop great looking glutes, but also maximise your performance and minimise your risk of injury. This book isn't the kind of "fad workout" you see popping up on social media. It gets right to the point and really targets the most important exercises you can do to develop your glutes so that they look great. The exercises will take time and dedication, but so do all the best things in life.

The glutes (your buttocks) are made up of three muscles. The gluteus maximus (largest), the gluteus medius (middle-sized) and the gluteus minimus (smallest). They work together to extend (straighten the legs), abduct (move the legs out to the side) and rotate the hips (to twist the legs inwards or outwards).

Gluteus Maximus

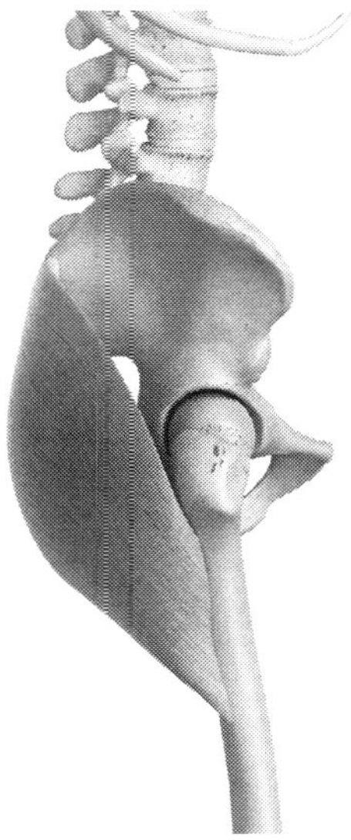

Gluteus Medius

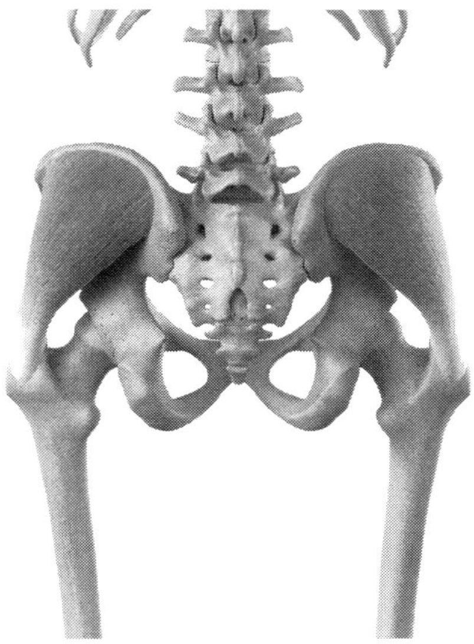

Gluteus Minimus

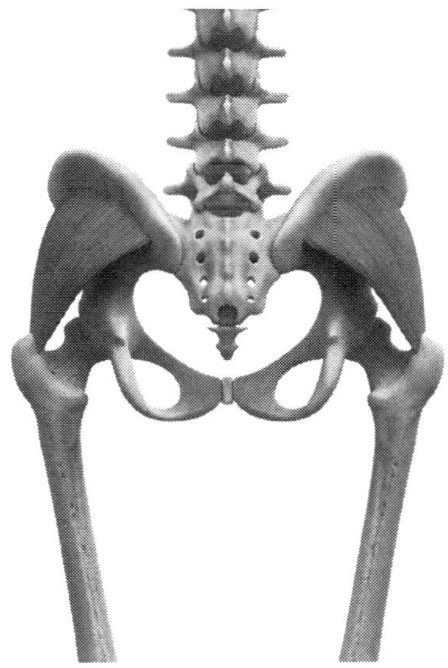

The glutes are the largest and strongest muscle mass in the body and they can provide both physical performance and great aesthetics.

The ability to forcefully and explosively extend your hips, for instance, is fundamental to sporting performance. Strong glutes will help you to run faster, jump higher, throw farther and strike harder.

The glutes also play a key role in maintaining the posture of the lumbar spine (lower spine) and pelvis, while preventing injuries by working to stabilise the lower back, hips, knees and ankles.

They really are the powerhouse of the human body, so spending time developing them properly is not only essential for looking great, you'll move better and feel better too.

Get the Videos

The videos to accompany each exercise are available to download for free from

https://fundamental-changes.teachable.com/p/top-40-glute-exercises/

or here

http://geni.us/betterbutt

Simply enrol in the course and you'll have free access to all 34 videos.

If you type above link into a browser, please note that there is no "www."

Equipment

Here is a list of the equipment required to complete all the exercises in this book. I've tried to keep it as simple as possible.

- Barbell (BB)
- Plates of varying weights that go on the barbell
- Dumbbells (DBs) of varying weights
- Kettlebells (KBs) of varying weights
- Weights bench
- Resistance bands of long and small loop bands

Any well-equipped gym, or even a home/garage gym, will contain all the equipment required, but I suggest buying your own set of resistance bands (long bands and small loop bands).

I recommend that you buy:

- A full set of long resistance bands (red, black, purple and green)
- A pack of 4-5 small loop bands of varying tensions

Many of the exercises in the book can be practised in the comfort of your own home, using bodyweight and resistance bands. Home workouts are included in Chapter Six: Programming.

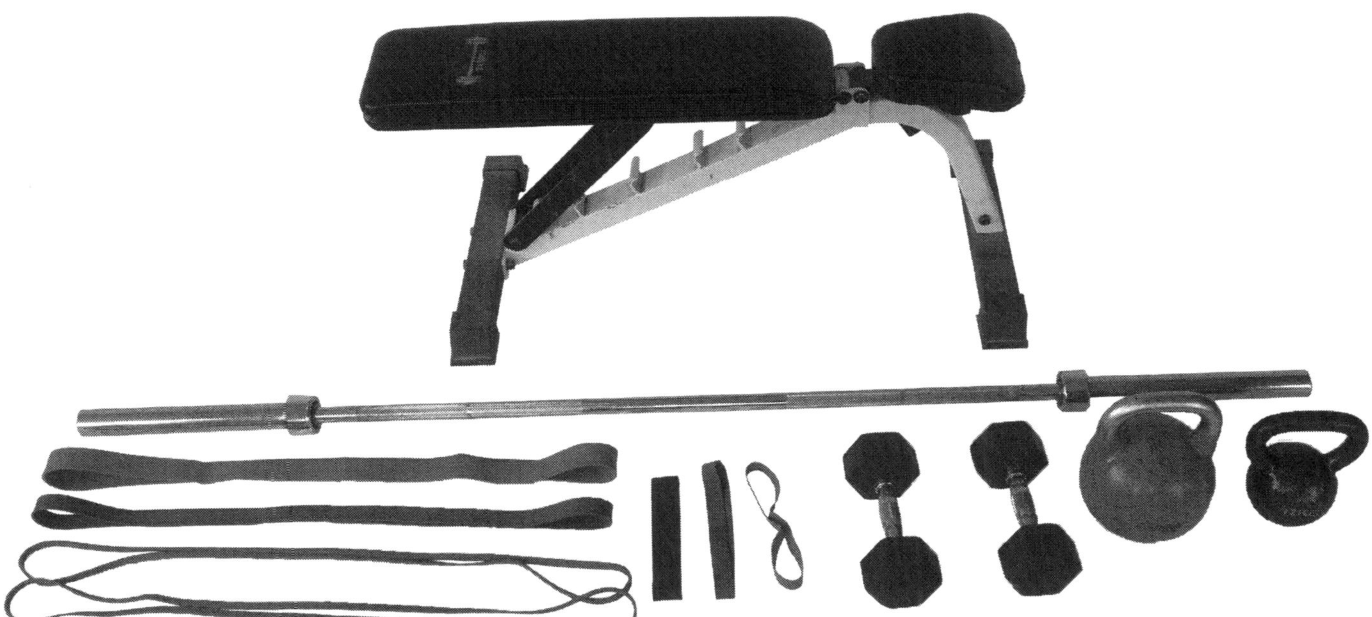

Chapter One: Glute Activation Exercises

Activation means "to get a specific muscle working".

If a muscle is not activating it means that it's not pulling its weight and requires targeted exercises to get it firing (contracting) as it should.

If the glutes are not firing properly, they will cause other muscles to over-compensate. This leads to imbalance, injury and an all-round reduction in performance.

This chapter contains ten effective activation exercises to perform *prior* to your session, or as *active recovery* in between training sessions. Active recovery is simply performing low-intensity exercises to help your muscles recover. Your blood carries nutrients that are vital for recovery, so gently increasing circulation speeds up the process.

If you suffer from delayed onset muscle soreness (DOMS) in the days after a workout, light walking or jogging may help to relieve it.

Activation drills are most commonly programmed with high reps to ensure that we get the muscle firing and help to ingrain the neuromuscular connection.

Hip Extension

This section consists of seven glute activation exercises that target hip extension (straightening the hips).

The seven exercises are my personal favourites for getting the gluteus maximus firing. I use them regularly with a wide array of clients in my strength and conditioning gym, and they always have great effect.

It is important to perform actions from different stances and positions, often using a variety of equipment. This both keeps things interesting, fun and helps to best engage the entire area.

The exercises in this chapter are done from standing, kneeling, quadruped and lying positions, and will be worked for high reps to create a deep burn in your gluteus maximus.

Your gluteus maximus is the muscle that makes up the bulk of your buttocks. Therefore, if you want to develop its size and shape, it is essential that it gets some attention!

Standing Band Kick Backs

Standing band kick backs are a simple exercise that can be performed with a small loop resistance band.

This exercise is incredibly easy to perform and it will create a beneficial burn in your glutes in no time at all.

1. Place a small loop band around your ankles.
2. You can perform the movement leaning into a wall or post or without support.
3. Kick one leg rearwards, while keeping both legs straight.
4. Squeeze your glutes hard at the top.
5. Bring your leg back down to the starting position (it doesn't have to touch the floor), before going into successive reps.
6. Complete 3-5 sets of 20-30 reps on each side.

Quadruped Hip Extensions

Quadruped hip extensions are an extremely effective glute exercise which work each side of the glutes independently (unilateral exercise).

This exercise (and similar variations to it) is often called "Donkey Kickbacks" and is one of the most commonly used exercises for glute development. It is a sure-fire way of building larger, better shaped and stronger glutes.

1. Kneel on all fours (quadruped position).
2. A small loop band can be used to increase the intensity of the exercise. Loop the band around your legs, just above your knees and clamp the band down under the knee of the non-working leg.
3. Begin the exercise by kicking one leg back, while maintaining the bent knee position.
4. Once your hip is fully extended, the sole of your foot will be facing the ceiling.
5. Squeeze your glutes hard at the top.
6. Bring your leg back down to the starting position (it doesn't have to touch the floor), before going into successive reps.
7. Complete 3-5 sets of 20-30 reps on each side.

Banded Glute Bridges

There's a good reason glute bridges are the most used gluteus maximus activation exercises – they are unbelievably efficient at getting the glutes working.

Lying down and driving your back into the floor as you extend your hips and squeezing your bum allows you to consciously concentrate on the muscles that should be working. This is known as "mind-muscle connection" and helps to increase glute engagement, while maintaining the optimal positioning of your lower spine. This a great exercise for those who suffer with lower back pain.

This exercise can be performed with or without a band. However, placing a band around your knees and driving them apart (abducting your legs), helps to maximise glute engagement as you extend your hips up from the floor.

1. Sit on the floor and place a small band around your legs, just above your knees.
2. Lie back, so your head is flat to the floor.
3. Place your hands to the side.
4. Bend your knees and bring your heels towards your glutes. This prevents your hamstrings from taking over the work.
5. Place your feet flat to the floor, either together or hip-width apart.
6. Coming up onto your heels will increase glute engagement.
7. Spread your knees apart to abduct and externally rotate your hips.
8. Squeeze your glutes and extend your hips.
9. Hold at the top for 1-3 seconds before returning to the starting position.
10. Complete 3-5 sets of 20-30 reps.

Single Leg Glute Bridges & Hip Thrusts

Single leg glute bridges are performed just like the previous exercise, however, one leg is raised off the floor, while the leg that is still on the floor performs the action.

Perform this exercise with your back elevated on a bench or raised platform (pictured). The back elevation turns the movement into a single leg hip thrust.

The single leg glute bridge is one of the most effective ways to test whether there is an imbalance between your right and left side. If things are imbalanced, one side will be more difficult or tire sooner. This is a great exercise to help balance both sides. If you find an imbalance, do some extra sets on the weaker side.

1. Lie with your back on the floor (glute bride) or place your mid-back (just below your shoulder blades) onto a bench (hip thrust). A band can also be placed just above the knees to increase the intensity of the exercise.
2. Place your hands to the side.
3. Bend your knees and bring your heels towards your glutes. This prevents your hamstrings from taking over the work.
4. Extend one of your knees, keeping it in line with the other knee.
5. Drive the foot that is still on the floor into the floor and squeeze your glute hard on that side to extend your hips.
6. Hold at the top for 1-3 seconds before returning to the starting position.
7. Complete 3-5 sets of 10-30 reps on each side.

Frog Pumps

Frog pumps are a simple variation of the glute bridge that can help to maximise glute engagement.

Frog pumps are essentially a glute bridge with a few tweaks to help maximise engagement. One of the ways frog pumps increase glute engagement is by having you perform high reps in an explosive manner. The gluteus maximus responds well to fast, explosive work.

The explosive nature of this exercise also makes it a great add-on to any metabolic conditioning (high intensity exercise) you do at the end of a strength workout.

1. Sit on the floor and lie onto your back.
2. Bend your knees. Keep your heels close to your glutes to reduce hamstring engagement.
3. Tilt your pelvis rearwards, bringing your lower back flat to the floor.
4. Flex your head slightly, bringing your chin to your chest, rather than keeping it flat to the floor.
5. Bend your elbows, clench your fists, and drive your arms into the floor.
6. Place the soles of your feet together and as close to your glutes as possible.
7. Squeeze your glutes and extend your hips.
8. A one-second pause can be added at the top. However, frog pumps are usually carried out quickly.
9. Complete 3-5 sets of 20-50 reps.

Banded Kneeling Hip Thrusts

Kneeling hip thrusts are an extremely effective way to get the glutes firing. They're not an exercise that you see often in the gym, but give them a go and you will absolutely love them!

1. Attach a medium to high tension resistance band (purple or green) around a solid structure (loop it through itself).
2. Step inside the band so that the band wraps around the crease of your hips.
3. Step forward to apply tension onto the band and kneel on the floor (shuffle forward while on your knees to increase the band tension).
4. Hinge at your hips so the band pulls your glutes rearward.
5. Contract your glutes and bring your hips into full extension.
6. Squeeze your glutes hard at the top.
7. Complete 3-5 sets of 20-30 reps.

Band Pull Throughs

Band pull throughs are a great exercise for your glutes as they create an explosive extension of your hips while in a standing position. This makes them an ideal activation prior to deadlifting as they help to instil lockout strength (the straightening of your hips during a deadlift).

1. Attach a medium to high tension resistance band (purple or green) around a solid structure and loop it through itself to secure it.
2. Stand with your back towards the band attachment point, place the band between your legs and hold the end.
3. Step forward to apply tension to the band.
4. Hinge at your hips, pushing your glutes rearwards. This will result in your arms reaching through your legs and behind you.
5. Holding the band tight in your hands, contract your glutes and bring your hips into full extension.
6. Squeeze your glutes hard at the top.
7. Complete 3-5 sets of 20-30 reps.

Hip Abduction

Although the gluteus maximus makes up the bulk of your buttocks, to achieve the best size and shape possible, you must ensure that all the glutes are developed, and that includes both the gluteus medius and minimus.

This section consists of four glute activation exercises that target hip *abduction*. Abduction means bringing the hip out to the side, away from the body. These exercises will be worked for high repetitions and will cause a deep burn in your gluteus medius and minimus (the side of your hip).

The glute medius is responsible for stabilising you while you are on one leg. If the glute medius is not pulling its weight, other muscles must compensate, and this can often lead to injuries. It is extremely beneficial to strengthen and build endurance in this muscle.

Fire Hydrants

Fire hydrants look quite easy, but they soon create an incredible burn in the side of the hips.

This is one of my favourite exercises for building the outer side of your buttocks.

1. Kneel on all fours (quadruped position).
2. A small loop band can be used to increase the intensity of the exercise. Loop the band around your legs, just above your knees and clamp the band down under the knee of the non-working leg.
3. Begin the exercise by kicking one leg out to the side, while maintaining the bent knee position (like a dog lifting its leg).
4. Try to keep your hips level – don't tilt away from the working leg to increase the range of motion (ROM).
5. Squeeze your glutes hard at the top.
6. Bring your leg back down to the starting position (it doesn't have to touch the floor), before going into successive reps.
7. Complete 3-5 sets of 20-30 reps on each side.

Clamshells

Clamshells have been a staple of gluteus medius development for years. Although the exercise can look a little silly, it can create an effective burn in the side of the hips.

The clamshell exercise can be made harder by adding bands to the movement. I prefer to work without added resistance and simply do a high number of reps. I often time the exercise rather than do a set number of reps, so it's an ideal drill to perform in front of the TV.

1. Lie on your side.
2. Bend your knees with your legs stacked on top of each other.
3. Ensure your hips are stacked on top of each other and that you are not leaning back. Leaning back during the movement results in other muscles getting involved and we want to isolate the glute medius.
4. Keep your feet together and raise the top knee upwards, away from the other knee. You should feel a contraction in the side of the top hip.
5. Bring the knee back towards the starting position and complete successive reps.
6. Complete 3-5 sets of 1-3 minutes on each side.

Side Lying Hip Abduction

Side lying hip abductions are similar to clamshells, except the working leg is kept straight. They can be performed with bodyweight as a timed exercise like the clamshell, or a small loop resistance band can be placed around the ankles to increase the intensity.

1. Lie on your side.
2. Your bottom leg can be bent. The top leg should be straight.
3. If using a small loop band, keep both legs straight and loop the band around your ankles.
4. Ensure your hips are stacked on top of each other and that you are not leaning back. Leaning back during the movement results in other muscles getting involved and we want to isolate the glute medius.
5. Raise the top leg off the bottom leg and point your toes towards the floor (pointing your toes towards the floor increases glute engagement).
6. Slowly raise the top leg up and down.
7. Complete 3-5 sets of 20-30 reps or work for 1-2 minutes.

Lateral Band Walks

Lateral band walks are a superb exercise to strengthen and build endurance in your gluteus medius.

This drill can be done with a short band placed around your feet to increase glute engagement. If you don't have a short band, place a long band around both feet and hold it at either end in each hand.

The lateral band walk is the exercise I use most for gluteus medius development, both personally and for most of my clients. It not only maximises the development of the glutes, but helps to build strength in the intrinsic muscles of the feet that help support your arches. In fact, collapsed arches are often a smoke signal for weak glutes.

Perform this exercise without your shoes on. This is something I recommend for most lower body stability exercises as it builds strength in your feet.

1. Loop the band under the arches of your feet.
2. Stand up tall with good posture, bend your knees slightly.
3. Step 1-2 foot-widths in the direction you are going. Stay in control and don't allow your leg to be dragged by the band.
4. Complete 3-5 sets of 10-20 strides in each direction.

Movement Pattern Warmup Exercises

Activation exercises are a key aspect of glute development. However, if you want to maximise your glute gains you need progress to larger movements that can be done with heavier weights. Although there are many important aspects to building muscle and strength, the intensity of exercise is fundamental. Basically, more weight = higher intensity.

The exercises in this section act as the ideal warm-up drills/technique work prior to performing the exercises in the following Bilateral Hip Extension chapter.

In this section I will teach you the bodyweight hip hinge and squat, both of which are integral for building glutes and overall strength development. I will also introduce my favourite exercise for developing squat technique, the *goblet squat*.

The hinge, squat and lunge are not only essential for strength development, but also for normal movement activities you perform on a daily basis. They make up three of the seven fundamental human movement patterns – hinge, squat, lunge, push, pull, rotate and gait.

Bodyweight Hinge

The hip hinge involves bending at your hips to allow your torso to drop forward, while maintaining a neutral spine (unbent and untwisted). Although it is fine to bend and twist your spine in the right situation, while working with heavy loads (deadlift) it is optimal to keep the spine in a neutral position.

The hinge is truly the foundation of good movement. People often think that you must perfectly squat down to correctly pick up an object, but this is unrealistic. There is nothing wrong with bending over (hinging at your hips) if the muscles that support the movement are working correctly and have the strength to accommodate the stress.

1. Stand with soft knees (slightly bent) and good upper body posture, ensuring your chest is proud (pushed out) and remains so throughout the movement.
2. Start by driving your glutes rearwards.
3. Standing a foot-length from a wall and attempting to touch the wall with your glutes works as an ideal teaching aid.
4. Maintain the soft knee position and keep driving your glutes back. This will cause your hips to hinge, dropping your torso forward.
5. Keep going until you feel your hamstrings reach the extent of their range of motion. Ensure you maintain a neutral spine.
6. Straight legs (soft knees) and a neutral spine will usually bring your torso parallel, or just above parallel, to the floor.
7. This movement can be performed with a medium-high tension band placed under your feet and around your neck. This exercise is referred to as a “banded good morning” and is an awesome glute activation exercise.
8. Complete 3-5 sets of 10-20 reps.

Bodyweight Squat

The ability to squat well is considered the epitome of functional movement and strength development. It is a fundamental movement that's used countless times a day.

You might think that you never squat, but every time you bend and straighten your knees and hips, you are working the same muscles.

Squats are the most effective way to developing your leg strength and, in turn, are an awesome exercise for your glutes.

In this section, I introduce the body weight squat and my personal favourite variation for teaching the movement – the goblet squat.

The strength of the legs is massive, so it is important to introduce weight to your training. A common phrase is "the mind will give in before the legs". This rings true because the legs are built to hold the weight of your body and potentially carry it for miles each day.

Things like joint anatomy and limb length can play a key role in the depth of your squat. I consider it ideal to squat just below parallel, where the crease of your hips is slightly lower than the top of your knee caps. This position maximises muscle engagement while placing the least stress on the rest of your body.

1. Take a shoulder-width stance with your toes pointing forwards or slightly outwards, but no more than 30 degrees.
2. Start the movement with your hips, driving your glutes backwards.
3. Bend your knees as your hips hinge (almost simultaneously).
4. Lower under control, keeping your knees in line with your toes. If your knees have a tendency to fall inwards (valgus), concentrate on pushing them outwards.
5. As you squat, bring your hands to the front. This acts as a counter balance as your centre of mass moves backward.
6. Squat down to the appropriate depth, ideally very slightly beyond your legs being parallel with the floor.
7. At full depth your knees should sit directly over your toes. Limb lengths can vary this, but you don't want your knees to move too far beyond your toes, as it places a lot of stress on them.
8. Use the stretch reflex (an involuntary contraction in response to a stretch in the muscles) to help you recoil out of the bottom of the squat, and drive back up out of the squat.
9. Complete 3-5 sets of 10-20 reps.

The Goblet Squat

The goblet is an awesome squat variation that helps to develop your squat mechanics. As you sit back into a squat, your centre of mass shifts rearwards, so holding a weight to your front is a perfect counter balance.

When novices perform squats with little depth and excessive forward tilt of their torso, coaches often try to rectify any perceived mobility issues the individual may have. However, stability, not mobility is often the underlying problem, as they compensate for their centre of mass shifting rearwards.

The goblet position makes a perfect counterbalance to the weight of the body moving backwards. The weight removes many of the stability/balance issues that might occur and allows for greater depth to be achieved on the squat, as the torso remains more upright. Adding the goblet weight can literally progress someone with a terrible bodyweight squat to squatting well, within one set. A kettlebell is usually used, but dumbbells or plates also work well.

1. Squat down and grab the horn (handle) of the kettlebell with both hands.
2. Lift the kettlebell and take a shoulder-width stance with your toes pointing forwards or slightly outwards (no more than 30 degrees).
3. Start the movement with your hips, driving the glutes back.
4. As your hips hinge, bend your knees (almost simultaneously).
5. Lower under control, keeping your knees in line with your toes.
6. Keep your elbows in, so that when you squat down, they comfortably fit in between your legs.
7. Once you have reached the appropriate depth (ideally, breaking parallel between your hamstrings and the floor), drive back up out of the squat.
8. Depending on the weight being used, complete 3-5 sets of 5-20 reps.

Chapter Two: Bilateral Hip Extension

Bilateral is the term used for exercises that use both sides of the body at the same time, like a squat.

The exercises in this section make up the foundation of your strength development and will allow you to lift the most weight.

When the aim is to develop a bigger, stronger, more powerful glutes, it is essential that you work the muscles intensely to build as much muscle fibre as possible, so the exercises in this section will normally be programmed for lower reps and heavier loads. The glutes respond to fast and hard contractions!

Regularly performing the exercises in this chapter and progressively increasing the weight used will result in huge glute development that maximises strength and perfects your size and shape.

The Valsalva Manoeuvre

During many of the exercises in this chapter, you will use the Valsalva manoeuvre when working with heavier loads. This is described as "a moderately forceful attempted exhalation against a closed airway" (like equalizing your ears on an airplane by blowing against a pinched nose).

The Valsalva manoeuvre, combined with a braced core, creates intra-abdominal pressure (IAP) and stabilises the spine. To visualise this, imagine the rigidity of a sealed plastic bottle full of air, compared to the rigidity an open bottle.

Another important concept to focus on is *mind-muscle connection*. This is the process of consciously thinking about the muscle you are working to increase its engagement. This technique should be used for all the exercises in this book.

Hip Thrusts – Barbell & Banded

Although the squat is an awesome glute exercise, hip thrusts allow you to concentrate on the final stages of hip extension. During a squat, a lot of emphasis is placed on straightening the knees, rather than just driving your hips forward and squeezing your glutes.

The hip thrust isolates hip extension while allowing huge weights to be lifted in relation to other glute isolation exercises.

This exercise can be performed with your upper back on the floor (glute bridge). However, the best way to perform the exercise is as a hip thrust with your upper back raised up.

The hip thrust is usually worked with heavy weights using the barbell. However, high tension resistance bands can also be used if you have the equipment to set them up i.e. rack with pegs / hip thrust machine or heavy dumbbells to clamp the bands down.

1. Set up a barbell with 45cm plates.
2. Rest your mid-back (just below your shoulder blades) against a bench. Often benches are a little high, so you can improvise with other platforms. In the picture I have used a truck tyre.
3. Roll the barbell up to the creases of your hips. A bar pad or folded mats are usually used as the position is quite uncomfortable on your hips.
4. Bend your knees so you can effectively drive the weight through your heels to maximise glute engagement.
5. Hold the bar with an overhand grip on the outside of your legs.
6. Contract your glutes and extend your hips, raising the barbell up.
7. Lower the barbell under control, either all the way to the floor (dead weight) or to just off the floor, and complete successive reps.
8. Depending on the weight being used, complete 3-5 sets of 5-20 reps.

Back Squat

The back squat is considered by most to be the king of the squats, as it is the variant that allows you to lift the most weight.

During the back squat, the barbell is held on your upper back in one of two positions. Experiment to find which is best for you.

High Bar Position: The barbell is held on the top of your upper traps, ensuring that it is *not* resting on the cervical vertebrae (distinct bony prominence on the back of the neck).

The barbell stays over your midfoot (halfway between your heel and toes, or the upper laces part of your trainer – about an inch in front of your shin) throughout the squat. If the barbell is high on your back, your torso requires less tilt to keep the barbell over the midfoot, so it stays more upright and allows for more depth.

During the high bar squat, leverage is weakest as you come to the position where your thighs are parallel with the floor. Make a conscious effort to drive your hips back under the barbell towards the end of the lift as this will bring you into a more mechanically efficient position. It maximises quad engagement and prevents your torso from falling forward.

Low Bar Position: The barbell is held 2-3 inches lower on your upper back, which will result in the barbell sitting behind your rear delts.

The reduced distance from your pelvis to the barbell can help to maximise the weight lifted. Therefore, competitive lifters often use a low bar position.

The low bar position requires a decent amount of shoulder mobility and can be uncomfortable if you are not used to it.

During a low bar squat, lifters will often use a *hip drive* method. Rather than driving your hips back under the barbell (which reduces the engagement of the hamstrings), you continue to drive upwards with your hips while maintaining a rigid back position (imagine driving upwards with your sacrum – upper buttocks).

Always do one or two warm-up sets with an unloaded barbell to get accustomed to the exercise. Find the style that feels natural for you.

The back squat is a complicated exercise that can cause injury if not done properly. Watch the video online at **http://geni.us/betterbutt** before attempting this by yourself.

1. Set the barbell on the rack at upper chest height.
2. Grab the barbell 1-2 palms wider than shoulder-width with a comfortable grip (either full or false grip).
3. A full grip will often feel more stable for the lifter. However, a false grip (thumbs on same side as your fingers) allows your wrists to stay in a more neutral position (as your elbows are pointing rearwards). Use the grip that suits you.
4. Move your head under the barbell, placing the barbell into your preferred position on your traps – high or low bar position.
5. Walk under the barbell, so that your hips are directly underneath to ensure you don't lift the barbell off the rack with your lower back.

6. Lift the barbell up off the rack with your legs and take 2-3 short strides rearwards – a long walkout wastes energy and increases the risk of injury.

7. Adopt your squatting stance. Experiment with various stance widths and see what feels best for you (hip joint structure often dictates which stance width feels best for you).

8. Take a big gulp of air, brace your core and use the Valsalva manoeuvre (a moderately forceful attempted exhalation against a closed airway. Like equalizing your ears on an airplane by blowing against a pinched nose).

9. As you brace your core, pull down on the barbell to help increase total body tension.

10. Initiate the squat with your hips, drive your glutes rearwards and bend your knees.

11. Allow your knees to track out directly over your toes (this will vary depending on limb length).

12. Sit back to the point where you break parallel and your hip crease dips just below the top of your knee caps, or as deep as you can go while maintaining good form.

13. Use the stretch reflex (involuntary contraction in response to a stretch in the muscles) to recoil out of the hole.

14. Drive your shoulders into the barbell and your feet into the floor.

15. Pull down hard on the barbell as if you are trying to bend it over your back. This helps to maximise total body tension and muscular engagement.

16. Drive back up out of the squat.

17. Once you reach the top of the lift, exhale and get ready for the next rep.

18. When working with heavy loads, it's important that you treat every rep as a single, perfectly performed movement.

19. Depending on the weight being used, complete 3-5 sets of 2-10 reps.

Box Squat

The box squat is one of my favourite squat variations as it places more load on the hips (glutes), while minimising the stress placed on the knees.

The box squat is a great exercise for those who find full squats to be stressful on their knees, or for those with knee injuries. In essence, a box is placed behind the legs, so you don't squat as far as with a full squat.

To maximise the benefits, the box should be at a height that requires your thighs to just break parallel with the floor, or to a depth which allows you to maintain optimal form. Again, please check out my demonstration video here **http://geni.us/betterbutt** before attempting the box squat.

1. Set up a barbell on the rack as you would for a back squat.
2. Place the box a small walkout distance behind you.
3. Take the barbell off the rack on your back and walk backwards towards the box.
4. Adopt a wide squatting stance.
5. Take a big gulp of air, use the Valsalva manoeuvre and contract your core muscles.
6. As you brace your core, pull down on the barbell to help increase total body tension.
7. Hinge at your hips and exaggerate the movement as you sit back with your glutes. Your shins should be vertical once you sit onto the box.
8. Don't fall back onto the box. Sit down slowly, maintaining total body tension as you meet the box.
9. Keep your heels down and don't lean back after you have sat down.
10. Once you have sat on the box for a second, maintain the tension in your torso and drive your shoulders into the barbell.
11. Once you drive your shoulders into the barbell, your feet will drive into the floor and your hips will start to raise upwards and forwards underneath the barbell.
12. Drive back up out of the squat.
13. Once you reach the top of the lift, exhale and get ready for the next rep.
14. When working with heavy loads, it's important that you treat every rep as a single, perfect movement.
15. Depending on the weight being used, complete 3-5 sets of 2-10 reps.

Romanian Dead Lift

The Romanian deadlift (RDL) was developed by a Romanian weightlifter called Nicu Vlad to strengthen his posterior chain (muscles on the rear of the body), specifically his back. The RDL is one of the best glute exercises and is a must for anyone who wants to increase their overall strength.

1. Start with the barbell at your hips (on a rack) with a pronated (over-hand) grip. Ensure you pick the barbell up with good form, while maintaining a neutral spine.
2. Initiate the movement by driving your glutes back and bending your knees slightly. Allow your shoulders to come over the barbell, while it maintains contact with your legs.
3. Keep driving your glutes back to facilitate the hinge and allow the barbell to track down your quads. If there is too much knee bend at this point, the barbell will sit on your quads, rather than track down smoothly.
4. Once the barbell passes your knee caps, bend your knees slightly to bring the barbell to about a palm's distance below your knees.
5. Engage the glutes and bring the barbell back up your legs, following the same path it went down. Maintain a vertical bar path throughout (if someone were watching from the side, they would see the barbell move in a vertical line).
6. Squeeze your glutes hard at the top to get them firing and proceed with successive reps.
7. Depending on the weight being used, complete 3-5 sets of 5-8 reps.

Conventional Deadlift

The deadlift is the king of the hinge and pull movements, and is the key to the development of strong, powerful hips and glutes.

Please note that lifting a heavy weight off the floor can stress your spine in a way that can cause injury. It is essential that you perform this exercise with good form. Once again, refer to the free videos at **http://geni.us/betterbutt**

It should be noted that injuries are not just a matter of technique or poor form. Regardless of whether you lift correctly or not, if your soft tissues haven't got the strength to handle the load (even with perfect form), injuries such as straining your lower back muscles can occur.

When it comes to the deadlift, many people are hell-bent on going as heavy as they can on every session, even if it's the first time they have lifted a barbell off the floor. To make real physical progression, you need to develop every link within the kinetic chain in your body and *progressive programming* will allow all your structures to adapt, remembering that some structures (particularly smaller muscles, tendons and ligaments involved in joint stabilisation) may not develop as quickly as others.

The lower back is one of the most important links within the kinetic chain. Without strength in this area we not only compromise performance, but also risk serious, life-changing injury.

Do not underestimate the importance of the lower back – it truly is an integral part of your ability to maintain posture and maximise performance.

1. Set the barbell up on the floor with 45cm plates.
2. Approach the barbell so that your midfoot is directly underneath it. Your shins should be an inch away from the barbell.
3. Hinge with your hips and bend your knees until you can grab the barbell.
4. Take an (over-hand) or alternated (one over-hand and one under-hand) grip.
5. Sit back with your glutes and drive your chest/ribcage up. This will bring your shins forward until they come into contract or are just off the barbell.
6. Take a big gulp of air, use the Valsalva manoeuvre, and brace your core musculature. As you do this, pull on the barbell slightly to create more tension and take away any slack between the barbell and plates.
7. Drive your heels into the floor and pull the barbell upwards and rearwards off the floor. Allow time for the inertia of the bar to be broken. You must produce enough force to break the weight off the floor, and this doesn't always happen as soon as you start pulling.
8. Once the barbell passes your knees, drive your hips into it and push your chest up. Your shoulders will fall naturally behind the barbell. There is no need to shrug or throw your shoulders rearwards.
9. Once you have finished locking out your hips, drive your glutes rearwards and bend your knees slightly to allow the barbell to track down your legs smoothly (just like the RDL).
10. Once the barbell passes your knee caps, bend your knees until the plates touch the floor.

11. At the bottom, exhale and get ready for the next rep.
12. Don't bounce the plates off the floor to create upward momentum. Treat every rep as a single, perfect movement.
13. Depending on the weight being used, complete 3-5 sets of 2-5 reps.

Sumo Deadlift

Sumo deadlifts are just like conventional deadlifts (pulling a dead weight off the floor), but your stance is wider and your hands are placed on the inside of the legs.

The sumo stance position results in a deadlift that places a little more load on your quads (thighs) rather than your back. The wider stance also creates more of a stretch on the glutes, which is great for glute development.

When it comes down to which deadlift variations you should use, it ultimately comes down to personal preference. We are all anatomically different, some hip joint structures are more suited to a wider stance, while others are suited to a narrower stance. Choose what works for you.

My recommendation is to cycle in both. Varying exercises maximises performance, minimises the risks of injury and keeps things interesting.

1. Set the barbell up on the floor with 45cm plates.

2. Approach the barbell and take a wide stance with your midfoot directly under the barbell.

3. You can keep your toes pointing forward (which can be less stressful on the hips). However, most lifters will push their toes outwards (externally rotate their hips).

4. The width of your stance is ultimately dependant on the flexibility of your adductors (groin). Some lifters will take an extremely wide stance where their toes are touching the plates at either side. However, most lifters will take a stance where their knees are sitting directly over their ankles, while in the bottom position.

5. Hinge with your hips and bend your knees until you can grab the barbell on the inside of your legs. This allows you to take a narrow, shoulder-width grip.

6. Take an (over-hand) or alternated (one over-hand and one under-hand) grip.

7. Sit back with your glutes and drive your chest/ribcage up. This will bring your shins forward until they come into contract or are just off the barbell.

8. Take a big gulp of air, use the Valsalva manoeuvre and brace your core musculature. As you do this, pull on the barbell slightly to create more tension and take away any slack between the barbell and plates.

9. Drive your heels into the floor and outwards as if you are spreading the floor apart. Pull the barbell upwards and rearwards off the floor. Allow time for the inertia of the barbell to be broken. You must produce enough force to break the weight off the floor, and this doesn't always happen as soon as you start pulling.

10. Once the barbell passes your knees, drive your hips into it and push your chest up. Your shoulders will fall naturally behind the barbell. There is no need to shrug or throw your shoulders rearwards.

11. Once you have finished locking out your hips, drive your glutes rearwards and bend your knees slightly to allow the barbell to track down your legs smoothly (just like the RDL, but in a wide stance – Sumo RDL).

12. Once the barbell passes your knee caps, bend your knees until the plates touch the floor.

13. At the bottom, exhale and get ready for the next rep.

14. Don't bounce the plates off the floor to create upward momentum. Treat every lift as an individual, perfectly performed movement.

15. Depending on the weight being used, complete 3-5 sets of 2-5 reps.

Sumo Deficit Squat

The sumo deficit squat involves standing on two raised platforms (usually plates) and squatting while holding a kettlebell or dumbbell between your legs.

The deficit (raised platform) allows you to squat to a full depth without the kettlebell touching the floor.

You will often feel your quads tire first when performing this exercise. Due to the loading position (to your front and below your hips), the exercise allows you to sit back into a deep squat. This creates a big stretch on the glutes and gets them working hard!

1. Create two raised platforms with plates at a width that puts you into a sumo stance (wide stance with your knees over your ankles at the bottom).
2. Pick up a kettlebell and hold it with straight arms so it falls between your legs.
3. Stand on the plates with your toes either pointing forward or out to the sides. Find what feels comfy for your hips.
4. Hinge at your hips and sit back with your glutes (exaggerate this). As you do this, bend your knees almost simultaneously.
5. Squat down to the depth your flexibility allows (you will feel a stretch in your groin), or the position which allows you to maintain optimal form.
6. Once at the bottom, drive your feet into the plates and stand back up.
7. Depending on the weight being used, complete 3-5 sets of 10-20 reps.

Kettlebell Swings

The kettlebell swing is a *ballistic* hip hinge movement that develops explosive hip extension and will help to build powerful hips. Ballistic movements perform maximum acceleration and velocity over short periods of time. It is essential that both the upward and downward phases of this lift are completed with good speed. The glutes love speed and power!

Ballistic movements are commonly associated with injuries, because during a fast movement it is harder to maintain control and more stress is placed on the soft tissues. It is important to remember that the actions we perform in sports, for example running, are generally ballistic in nature, so it's important to incorporate these actions into your training.

There are two main styles of swing: the Russian swing, which brings the kettlebell to chest height, and the American swing, which brings the kettlebell overhead.

We will be using the Russian swing.

The true purpose of the kettlebell swing is to create an explosive extension of the hips. Once the kettlebell reaches chest height, you have achieved full extension in the hips and raising the kettlebell any higher simply takes away from the exercise. If the kettlebell easily surpasses chest height, grab a heavier weight to maximise muscle recruitment.

At the bottom of the lift (where the kettlebell is between your legs), your knees should be slightly bent. The kettlebell swing does not involve a squatting action.

It works well to exhale at the bottom of the movement, while your ribcage and stomach are compressed, and inhale at the top of the movement, while your rib cage is expanded.

1. Place the kettlebell an arm's length in front of you.
2. Take a shoulder-width or slightly wider stance with soft knees. Hinge at the hips and drive your glutes rearwards. This will bring your torso just above parallel to the floor.
3. Grab the horn (handle) of the kettlebell.
4. Explosively pull the kettlebell rearwards into the *back swing* (kettlebell swung between your legs). Your arms should be high in your groin. If they are not, stress is placed on your lower back, rather than spread through your glutes and hamstrings.
5. Once the kettlebell has reached the end of the back swing, explosively contract your glutes and hamstrings to fire the kettlebell up to chest height.
6. From chest height, allow the kettlebell to swing back down in a fast, but controlled manner. Perform a full back swing (keeping your arms high in your groin) and continue with successive reps.
7. Depending on the weight being used, complete 3-5 sets of 5-20 reps.

Back Extensions – GHD or 45 Degree Hyper

The most effective way to perform back extensions is on a GHD (Glute and Hamstring Developer). These machines allow you to maximise the work on the glutes.

It is important not to overstress the spine by hyperextending at the top. However, the glutes really do come into their own during hip hyperextension. Raising your torso slightly beyond the height of your legs and consciously squeezing your glutes will help you to maximise glute engagement.

This exercise will work your entire posterior chain (calves, hamstrings, glutes and back muscles). However, we can alter the positioning slightly to maximise the work on the glutes. Using bent knees will slacken the hamstrings and place more emphasis on the glutes.

1. Set up the GHD so that with straight or slightly bent knees, your hips sit just to the front of the pad.
2. Place your thighs on the pad with your knees slightly bent and your toes pointed outwards.
3. Allow your torso to drop forwards over and below the pad.
4. Contract your posterior chain (specifically your glutes) to raise your torso back up in line with your legs. It is fine to hyperextend at the top, but be careful not to place too much stress on the lower spine.
5. The movement can be loaded by holding a plate at your chest, or even by putting a barbell on your back.
6. Complete 3-5 sets of 10-20 reps.

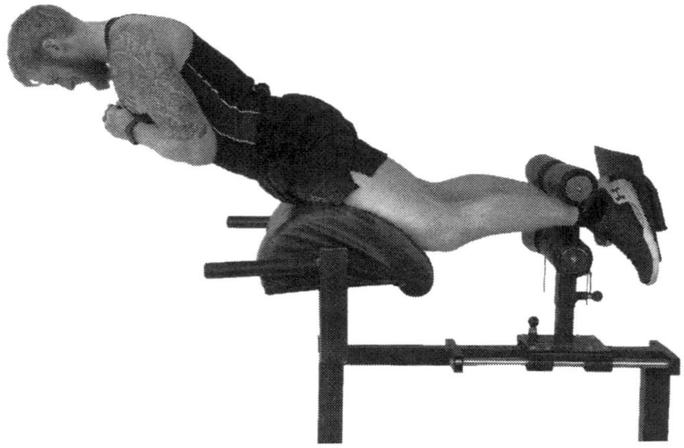

Reverse Hypers

Reverse hypers work the muscles of the posterior chain (glutes, hamstring and back muscles) just like back extensions on the GHD. Rather than moving your torso, the torso remains still while the legs move up and down. They allow you to safely work hip hyperextension, creating a brutal glute exercise.

A reverse hyper machine is ideal for the exercise, although most gyms don't own one, so I will show you how to perform the movement on a bench. I like to set the bench at a moderate incline, so the full ROM (range of motion) can be worked.

1. Set the bench at a moderate incline.
2. Lie chest down over the top of the bench so that your head is towards the seat. This will result in your legs hanging off the top of the bench (the top of the bench will be against the creases of your hips).
3. Contract your glutes and raise your legs up in line with your torso. Ensure that if you hyperextend slightly at the top, you don't put unnecessary stress on your lower spine.
4. A small loop band can be placed around your ankles (push your legs outwards – abduct) to increase the engagement of the glutes.
5. Complete 3-5 sets of 10-20 reps.

Chapter Three: Unilateral Hip Extension

Anyone who has programmed single leg exercises into their training regime will know just how effective they are at getting the glutes working. Just be aware of the muscle soreness that can be created by a heavy single leg session; you can be sore for days!

Unilateral is the term used for exercises which work one side of the body at a time, for example, a lunge.

During many daily activities and sporting actions we are required to work while on one leg – for example walking and running. It is essential that we develop stability and the ability to accommodate stresses placed through the legs by developing single leg strength.

Single leg strength is not only essential for daily human function, sporting performance and injury prevention, but is also the key to developing your glutes aesthetically.

Single Leg Box Squat

The single leg box squat is a great glute exercise and stability drill for the hips and knees.

The exercise can be performed on a box or bench and the depth of the squat can be tailored to your ability level (stacked plates can be used to increase or decrease depth). The movement is usually worked to a parallel or slightly below squat depth.

1. Stand in front of a box or bench.
2. Take one leg off the floor and hold it slightly to the front. This leg will stay off the ground throughout the movement.
3. Sit rearwards onto the bench (you can start the movement from the seated position, if it suits you better).
4. Concentrate on controlling the eccentric (downward) phase of the squat. Ensure the knee of the weight-bearing leg doesn't fall inwards (valgus) and keep the knee rearwards of your toes. During box squats, your shin will maintain a more vertical angle.
5. Once your glutes touch the bench, keep tension and drive up through your heel into the standing position.
6. A weight can be held to the front. This will increase the intensity of the movement, but also help to counterbalance the squat. A squat is often much easier with a small weight held to the front.
7. Complete 3-5 sets of 5-10 reps on each side.

Rear Foot Elevated Split Squats (RFESS)

The next few exercises in this book are described as *split squats* and *lunges*.

The split squat and lunge appear very similar at first glance, but there is a small difference.

During a split squat, only one leg is used to complete the movement while the other leg is at rest, applying a small degree of support.

During a lunge, both legs, regardless of their position, are involved in completing the movement. Usually the front "plant" leg holds around 75% of the weight, while the rear supporting leg is holding around 25%.

The RFESS is one of the most commonly used split squat variations, because it is an outstanding exercise to build leg strength and develop the glutes.

The RFESS involves a rear leg elevation that's usually done on a bench at knee or upper shin height. I often program this exercise using a 4-8-inch elevation. This smaller leg elevation allows for more weight to be loaded to the exercises, while the higher elevation (on a bench) requires a little more stability. Try various heights and see what works well for you.

This exercise can be performed with a barbell or dumbbells held at either side in a farmer's carry position.

1. Stand in front of a raised platform (plates or bench) and take one long stride forward.
2. Place the nonworking leg onto the raised platform. Either on your toes or by placing the laces part of your trainers down. Find what feels comfy for you.
3. If you are too close to the platform, the knee of your working leg will track too far forward, which will place excess stress on the knee. If you are too far forward, it will restrict mobility and therefore restrict the depth you can achieve – hop forward or rearwards to find the optimal position if needed.
4. Squat down with the front leg until the knee of your rear leg is just off the floor.
5. Drive your heel into the floor and raise back up to the starting position before completing successive reps.
6. Depending on the weight being used, complete 3-5 sets of 5-10 reps on each side.

Front Foot Elevated Split Squats (FFESS)

Performing alternating FFESS is a fantastic way to help mobilise the pelvis. A front foot elevation of 5-10 inches allows you to do this effectively without placing too much stress on the knees.

The FFESS not only effectively works the quads, glutes and hamstrings, but also acts to stretch the hip flexor of the rear leg, which can often be too tight. Tight hip flexors can cause lower back pain and result in reduced performance by restricting hip extension.

This exercise can be performed with a barbell or dumbbells held at either side in a farmer's carry position.

1. Stand in a hip width stance, a long stride rearward from a 5-10 inch platform.
2. Stride forward with one leg and place your whole foot flat on the platform, ensuring your knee doesn't track too far forward.
3. Lower yourself into a single leg squat, concentrating the load onto your front leg, while your rear leg provides support.
4. Lower to a depth that facilitates a stretch on the rear hip flexor, but not to a point where the stretch on the rear leg becomes detrimental to your ability to load the exercise.
5. Rise up and stride backwards to the starting stance. Complete successive reps using alternating legs.
6. Depending on the weight being used, complete 3-5 sets of 4-10 reps on each side.

Walking, Reverse & Deficit Revers Lunges

Lunges can be performed forwards, backwards and laterally out to the side, either moving in one direction (walking lunge) or in an alternating fashion where you return to the same starting position each time.

A forward stride into a lunge is most often used simply because it is what comes naturally. However, a forward striding lunge can place undue stress on the front knee. If you have knee pain or find the forward lunge stressful, I recommend using a backwards stride (reverse lunge), which helps reduce the strain.

In this exercise, I suggest using a *semi-inline stance*, where the feet line up to the side of each other with little or no gap between them from a front view. It's fine to go wider than this if you require extra stability, but an excessively straddled stance can apply stress to your groin.

The semi-in-line stance provides a stable foot placement, while maintaining optimal mechanics for the hip joints and the musculature of the lower body.

This exercise can be performed with a barbell or dumbbells held at either side in a farmer's carry position.

Walking Lunge:

1. Place your feet a hip-width apart.
2. Take a reasonably long stride forward with your right leg. This will allow your left knee to drop comfortably towards the floor while your right knee tracks forward slightly, but is still behind your toes.
3. It is fine for your left knee to gently touch the floor. However, this is often avoided to ensure tension remains throughout your body and you don't strike your knee causing bruising. I suggest keeping your knee 1 inch off the floor.
4. As you stride with the front leg and your knee bends, a slight hip hinge will ensure the movement maximises the engagement of not only your quads, but also your hamstrings and glutes. This also ensures your knee doesn't move too far forward.
5. During walking lunges, you can set the recovering leg down before striding out with it into the next lunge, or pass it straight past the supporting leg and into the next lunge.
6. Depending on the weight being used, complete 3-5 sets of 4-10 reps on each side.

Reverse & Deficit Reverse Lunges:

1. Place your feet a hip-width apart on a raised platform, as if performing a deficit lunge (pictured).
2. Take a reasonably long stride rearward with your right leg. This will allow your right knee to drop comfortably towards the floor while your left knee bends but stays in the same position. The front knee doesn't track forward over the toes, so there is reduced stress on the knee joint.
3. Once you have reached the optimal depth (knee around an inch off the floor), stride back up onto the raised platform and stride rearward with the opposite leg.
4. Depending on the weight being used, complete 3-5 sets of 4-10 reps on each side.

Lateral Lunges

The lateral lunge is a lunge variation where you stride out to the side keeping the non-striding leg straight.

This variation both mobilises and strengthens your adductors (inside of your thighs), which are normally overlooked when it comes to training. They also work the glutes intensely.

The lateral lunge can be performed from a pre-set starting position where your legs are spread at the distance required to lunge with good form, or you can start from a hip-width stance and stride sideways into the wider stance before dropping into the lunge.

I recommend using a kettlebell in a goblet position if you want to add weight.

1. Take a wide stance. This may need adjusting when you try the first rep.
2. Keep your toes forward facing and stay on the soles of your feet throughout the whole movement.
3. Bend your left knee and drive your glutes back to facilitate a hinge.
4. Full depth is achieved when you feel a full stretch on your adductors. Don't roll onto the side of your right foot.
5. Depending on the weight being used, complete 3-5 sets of 4-10 reps on each side.

Crossover Lunges

Crossover lunges involve a rotational movement at the hips during the lunge which creates a nice stretch on the glutes and maximises the effectiveness of the movement.

Adding rotational exercises into your training is essential, as most of the exercises we perform involve flexion and extension movements that can cause us to become stiff in others i.e. rotation.

The movement can be performed with a barbell on your back, or while holding a weight to the front in a goblet position.

1. Start with a shoulder-width stance.
2. Lunge rearwards and off to the right with your left leg. This will turn your hips slightly to the left and bring your left foot to the rear and off to the right-hand side of your right leg.
3. Land on the ball of your left foot and drop your left knee towards the floor.
4. It is fine for your left knee to gently touch the floor. Exercise caution as this is often avoided to ensure tension remains throughout your body, and that you don't bruise your knee. I suggest keeping your knee 1 inch off the floor.
5. Stride back up to the starting position and complete the same action on the opposite side.
6. Depending on the weight being used, complete 3-5 sets of 4-10 reps on each side.

Step-Ups

Climbing stairs is essentially a more powerful version of walking and requires far more muscular engagement. When we increase the height of the step and add weight, it becomes a truly awesome exercise, not only for the glutes, but for overall conditioning too.

This exercise can be performed with a barbell, but is most commonly performed with dumbbells.

Step-ups are usually done at around knee height, but the higher the step-up the greater the glute engagement.

1. Stand a foot-length behind the box.
2. Stride upwards with your right leg, placing your entire foot on the box.
3. Drive your right foot into the box and stride up with your left leg.
4. Once standing straight on the box, you can step back down, leading with your right leg.
5. A variation is to not place your left leg down, but drive your left knee up to hip height instead. This variation maximises hip extension on your right side and requires more stability.
6. Once back on the floor, this constitutes 1 rep.
7. Alternate the leading leg between each rep, or lead with your right leg for half the reps, before completing the final half with your left leg.
8. Complete 3-5 sets of 4-10 reps on each side.

Single Leg Romanian Dead Lift

Single leg RDL's follow the same action as the RDL seen in Chapter Two (a hinge at the hips with a slight bend of the knee). During the single leg RDL, the movement is carried out on one leg while the other swings to the rear.

The exercise is usually performed with a dumbbell in each hand. I like to perform the exercise with a dumbbell in the opposite hand to the leg I am working. Doing this with heavier loads for high reps will create an incredible burn in your glutes!

Although the single leg RDL is designed to build stability in the hips, I often allow clients to support themselves slightly with their free hand on a wall or post if they are unable to keep their balance.

1. Grab one or two dumbbells.
2. Stand on one leg with the other leg cocked rearwards.
3. Hinge at your hips and lower the dumbbell(s) towards the floor.
4. Throughout the movement, maintain a neutral spine.
5. As the dumbbell passes your knee caps, bend your knees slightly before contracting your posterior chain and bring yourself back to the starting position.
6. Squeeze your glutes hard at the top.
7. Depending on the weight being used, complete 3-5 sets of 10-20 reps on each side.

Chapter Four: Conditioning Exercises

One of the best ways to finish a workout and push a muscle group to its limits is to end your session with a *metabolic finisher*. This is a short, intense workout that you perform at the end of your session to ensure you are completely burnt out (in a good way).

In this section I have chosen three exercises that work the glutes hard, while building your cardio-respiratory fitness.

The exercises in this section can be combined back-to-back to create a brutal metabolic finisher. See the metabolic finisher table in Chapter Six: Programming, for more information.

There is no single way to the development of any muscle – the real key is to hit it from all angles. In this book we began with glute activation exercises, progressed to bilateral and unilateral strength, and will end with exercises that can be incorporated into your metabolic conditioning (cardio).

The wide selection of exercises allows you to effectively increase the frequency, volume and intensity of the glute work in your training regime. These approaches will create the results you want to see and are explained in greater depth in Chapter Six: Programming.

Jump Squats – Conventional & Wide-Narrow

Any jumping action requires huge activation from the glutes to propel your body off the floor. This makes jump squats an awesome glute exercise. The jumping actions also make jump squats one of the most physically demanding exercises on both your leg muscles and cardio-respiratory system.

Conventional Jump Squats

1. Take a shoulder width or slighter wider stance as you would for a bodyweight squat.
2. Squat down to a parallel, or just below parallel, position before recoiling quickly into a full jump.
3. Cushion your landing by going straight into the next squat, or bend your knees slightly to cushion your landing before going into the next rep.
4. Complete 3-5 sets of 10-20 reps.

Wide-Narrow Jump Squats

1. Take a narrow stance, either hip-width or slightly narrower. A narrow stance will limit mobility/stability, so go as narrow as you can go without your heels raising as you squat.
2. Perform a narrow stance squat and drive upwards into a full jump.
3. Land in a wide stance – ideally a wide stance that still allows you to hit a parallel squat position.
4. Perform a wide stance squat and drive upwards into a full jump.
5. Continue to alternate between the narrow and wide jump squat.
6. If you need a short break to reset between each rep, ensure you bend your knees slightly upon landing to cushion the impact.
7. Complete 3-5 sets of 5-20 reps – 1 rep = 1 of each squat.

Jump Lunges

Jump lunges require good stability and can be regressed by reducing the amount that the rear knee drops. To maximise the intensity on the glutes, dropping the knee to just above the floor is ideal.

1. Stride into the bottom of a lunge position – it is easier to start from this position.
2. Jump upwards, switch your feet, and land in the bottom of the opposite lunge position.
3. Ensure your rear knee does not strike the ground and that you take a long enough stride so that your front knee does not track too far forwards.
4. If a full jump lunge requires too much stability, reduce the intensity by starting from a higher lunge position (rear knee higher off the ground).
5. Complete 3-5 sets of 5-20 reps – 1 rep = 1 repeat on each side.

Side Skaters

Side skaters incorporate more lateral and rotational movement. This is great for both glute development and the maintenance of healthy hips, pelvis and lower back.

1. Take a hip/shoulder-width stance.
2. Bound to the right, landing on your right leg only and bring your left leg round to the rear and sideways past the right leg.
3. Once the toes of the left foot touch the floor, or come to a position just off the floor, bound to the left and land on your left leg, bringing your right leg round to the rear and sideways past the left leg.
4. Keep repeating the same action for successive reps.
5. Complete 3-5 sets of 5-20 reps – 1 rep = 1 repeat on each side.

Chapter Five: Glute Releases & Stretches

The three muscles of the glutes are an area that needs extra attention when it comes to strength. They often become tense (when overworked or weak), causing pain in your buttocks, low back and hamstrings.

Prolonged sitting can also cause the glutes to become tense, which can often lead to back pain.

An important muscle to consider when working on the glutes is the piriformis. The piriformis is a small muscle located under your glutes. The sciatic nerve travels either underneath or through the piriformis.

The piriformis can often become tense due to weakness or through overuse, especially if your main gluteal muscles don't fire as well as they should.

When the piriformis becomes stressed, it can be a literal pain in your butt, and due to the location of your sciatic nerve can result in sciatic pain that shoots down the leg from the lower back.

Release techniques are hands-on therapy that you can perform yourself, usually with a foam roller or massage ball. The aim of these techniques is to use pressure to stimulate a sensory receptor called the Golgi tendon organ that tells the muscle fibers to relax.

These techniques will not stimulate a long-term change in muscle tension by themselves. Instead, they will cause a short-term release of muscle tension, which in turn will allow you to gain a more effective stretch to the tissues.

Release techniques are highly effective for the glutes and piriformis. Caution should be practised when working on the glutes, due to the location of the sciatic nerve. Driving a massage ball into your sciatic nerve can potentially leave you with worse symptoms than those you are trying to relieve.

I do not recommend using release techniques on this area if you are suffering from sciatic pain or are not certain how you can safely manipulate the soft tissues.

Foam Rolling Glutes

This is a great release technique for the glutes. Caution must be practised not to irritate the sciatic nerve.

1. Place a foam roller or massage ball on the floor. A foam roller will help to distribute the pressure across the gluteal area and so will be less intense.
2. Place your upper gluteal area on the foam roller (where your back pockets would be).
3. To roll your right-hand side, place your right leg over your left, so that the ankle of your right leg is just above your left knee. This lengthens the musculature being worked.
4. If this is not possible, simply drop your right knee off to the side.
5. Slowly roll up and down the muscle mass for 30-60 seconds.
6. Complete 1-2 times on each side.

Seated Glute Stretch

This stretch for your glutes and piriformis can easily be done at your desk.

1. Sit upright in your chair.
2. To stretch your right side, place your right leg over your left, so the ankle of your right leg is just above your left knee.
3. Keeping your chest proud, lean towards your right knee. Don't round your spine and bend your head down towards your knee, instead push your chest forward with a neutral spine.
4. Hold for 30-60 seconds, or for 2 minutes if the musculature is very tense.
5. Complete 1-3 times on each side.

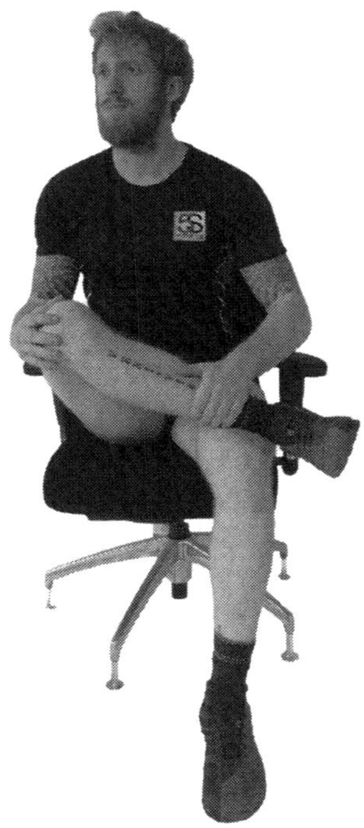

Figure Four Stretch

This is my favourite glute stretch as it's a comfortable position to hold what can be an intense stretch for longer periods of time. It definitely helps you to increase your flexibility.

1. Lie on your back.
2. To stretch your right side, raise your left leg up with your knee bent at 90 degrees.
3. Place your right leg over your left, so the ankle of your right leg is just below your left knee.
4. Reach through and grab round the back of your left leg with both hand and pull towards your chest.
5. Hold for 30-60 seconds, or for 2 minutes if the musculature is very tense.
6. Complete 1-3 times on each side.

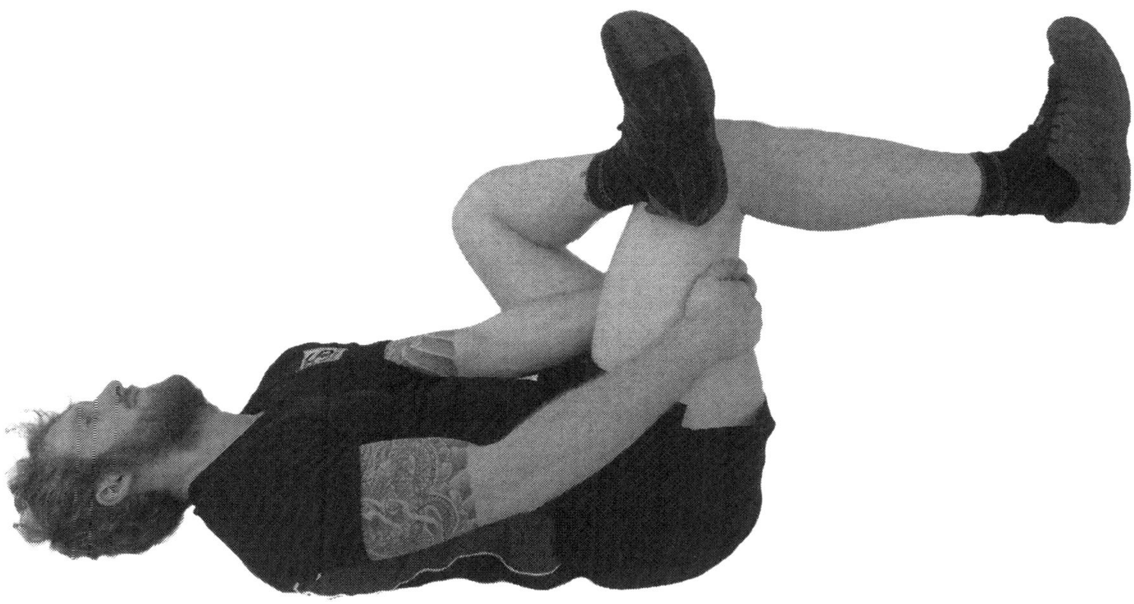

Pigeon Stretch

The pigeon stretch is a little more advanced than the previous two stretches. It makes the ideal progression for anyone who wants to increase their mobility further.

1. Start on all fours.
2. To stretch your right side, place the outer side of your right leg onto the floor. The sole of your right foot will be pointing to the left, while your knee is pointing to the right.
3. Slide your left leg back as you move your right leg into position.
4. Keep your hips forward-facing and your chest proud, driving your chest upwards to increase the stretch.
5. If you can, keep your right foot in line with your right knee. However, you might need to pull your foot back towards your hip.
6. Hold for 30-60 seconds, or for 2 minutes if the musculature is very tense.
7. Complete 1-3 times on each side.

Chapter Six: Programming

This chapter takes the information from the previous sections and brings it together to create effective workout programs.

Although many of the programs in this section are simple glute workouts, I have also included more detailed programming that consists of the larger compound movements (which work multiple joints and muscle groups) such as the squat. Below is a brief overview of the most effective ways to programme resistance training.

How to Program

Training Variables:

Step 1: The first variable you need to consider is how many times a week you will be training – this is your Training Frequency.

Step 2: Choose the movements you will train – this is your Exercise Selection.

Step 3: Choose the order of the exercises.

The ideal way to order them is to start with primary lifts, move on to assistance lifts, and finish with auxiliary lifts.

Primary Lifts are compound exercises. They are of utmost importance in terms of exercise selection as they work movements fully and require the most effort.

Assistance Lifts are often referred to as accessory exercises and are also compound movements. They are chosen to develop specific movements or muscle groups that help you to perform primary lifts or specific sporting actions.

Auxiliary Lifts are single joint exercises. They are chosen to help develop your ability to perform primary lifts or specific sporting actions.

Step 4: Choose the volume and intensity you are going to be working at on each exercise i.e. How many sets and reps you will be performing (volume), and what weight you are working at (intensity).

The intensity of an exercise is usually increased by raising the weight being lifted, but it can also be increased by making the exercise mechanically harder. For example, increasing the range of motion (ROM), or adopting a position that is less efficient (a narrower grip on a bench press).

You can also increase the intensity by varying the speed of the lift. Training Density is the work you can do in each amount of time. For example, 5x10 reps in 20 minutes has a lower density than 10x10 reps in 20 minutes.

Step 5: Choose the rest periods you will take between sets and between each exercise.

The main purpose of rest periods is to allow your breathing and heart rate to reduce. This allows substances that may impede training intensity to clear, while allowing substances that provide energy to be restored.

Another important aspect of rest is to allow time for your nervous system to recover. This is especially important in strength training, specifically when working at maximal loads. When strength training, you need to take sufficient rest periods to allow you to facilitate optimal work on each set, without taking so long that the fatigue from previous sets has completely worn off. In other words, successive sets should have a cumulative effect.

Recommended rest periods:

(Percentages are explained in the next section)

• When working above 85% of your 1RM, take 3-5 minutes rest between sets.

• When working between 70-85%, take 2-3 minutes rest between sets.

• When working below 70%, take 1-2 minutes rest between sets. However, anywhere up to 3 minutes on assistance work is fine, if needed. Rest periods can be dynamic, depending on how you feel.

• When performing dynamic effort sets, take 40-60 seconds rest between sets.

• Core work is best performed with short rest periods of between 10-30 seconds.

Step 6: Smash your session!

Quantifying your Programming:

The easiest way to quantify your program is to test your *one repetition maximum* or 1RM on the *primary lifts* (a *training max* is a 1RM with no breakdown in form, which is what I work off). You can then work off percentages of the 1RM.

Working off percentages isn't perfect, and I suggest allowing for 5% on either side to account for good and bad days. However, percentage work is a great way to quantify the weight you are lifting.

Testing a 1RM can be quite stressful and comes with a certain risk of injury, especially if you are not an experienced lifter.

Due to this risk, coaches also work off an athlete's 2, 3 and 5RM, which are all much less stressful to test. To estimate 1RM from 2, 3 or 5RM, we use formulas or coefficients (although 1RM apps can be downloaded to your phone).

A coefficient is a constant number that is multiplied by the variable (weight lifted). These coefficients have been worked out over various studies and are surprisingly accurate.

The coefficient for a 5RM is 1.16 – so if your 5RM is 100kg, multiply that weight by 1.16 to find your 1RM. In this case, the 1RM would be 116kg.

Different coefficients and formulas give negligibly different results, but they all work well as estimations from which to program.

Another method to quantify your programming is the *rating of perceived exertion* (RPE) scale. This is simply a scale which rates your perceived level of physical effort. The simplest scale is a 1-10 rating with 1 being almost no exertion, 5 being moderate exertion, and 10 being the hardest it could possibly be for the number of reps programmed.

If I were to program 4x8 lunges at RPE 10, it means I want the lunges to be as hard as they possibly can be for the programmed reps. Whereas, if I programmed 4x5 single leg RDLs at RPE 6, it means I don't want the intensity to be too high, as I want to concentrate on stability and performing the exercise well.

Recording your RPE allows you to rate how hard each set is on the day. If you look back 3 weeks and see that you performed 5 reps on a back squat at 80kg, which was 80% of your 1RM, that's great information. But if you add an RPE, you can see whether it was RPE 10 or RPE 7 for example. If it was RPE 7, you know you can potentially push to 85% for 5.

Rep Max Estimations:

2RM = 95% of 1RM

3RM = 90-92% of 1RM

5RM = 85-87% of 1RM

8RM = 80-82% of 1RM

10RM = 75% of 1RM

These are estimations and can vary from person to person. For example, a female who has great endurance but less capacity for maximal effort lifting may be able to perform 5x5 at 95% of her 1RM. Whereas a male who has comparatively poor muscular endurance, but is an experience maximal effort lifter, may struggle with 5x5 at 80% of their 1RM.

These estimations can also vary on different lifts (squats, deadlifts, presses). This is due to your lower body having different capacities to your upper body, for example.

My Recommendations for Working Sets:

- Sets of 2 reps – work at 90%+ of your 1RM
- Sets of 3 reps – work at 85%+ of your 1RM
- Sets of 5 reps – work at 75-80+% of your 1RM
- Sets of 10 reps – work at around 70% of your 1RM

Warming Up for Resistance Training:

The RAMP warmup protocol is ideal prior to resistance sessions (explained in the *how to use* section). However, warming up with light sets of the primary movement and progressively loading up is often sufficient.

An example of progressively loading up for the back squat could be:

- 1-2 Sets with an unloaded barbell (5-10 Reps).
- 1 Set at 60% of the maximum weight you will be working at (5-10 Reps).
- 1 Set at 80% of the maximum weight you will be working at (3-5 Reps).
- Begin your 1st set of the programmed weight.

Sample Programs

Mobility Regime:

Exercise	Sets/Reps/Time	Rest	Notes
Foam Rolling Glutes	2x60-90 Seconds - Each side	10 Seconds	
Figure Four Stretch	2x1-2 Minutes – Each Side	10 Seconds	
Pigeon Stretch	2x1-2 Minutes – Each Side	10 Seconds	

Glute Activation 1:

Exercise	Sets/Reps/Time	Rest	Notes
Banded Glute Bridges	3x20 Reps	20-30 Seconds	
Lateral Band Walks	3x20 Strides in Each Direction	20-30 Seconds	
Band Pull Throughs	3x20 Reps	20-30 Seconds	

Glute Activation 2:

Exercise	Sets/Reps/Time	Rest	Notes
Single Leg Glute Bridges	3x15 Reps – Each Side	20-30 Seconds	
Fire Hydrants	3x10 Reps – Each Side	20-30 Seconds	
Banded Kneeling Hip Thrusts	3x20 Reps	20-30 Seconds	

Full Glute Workout 1:

Exercise	Sets/Reps/Time	Rest	Notes
Banded Glute Bridges	3x20 Reps	20-30 Seconds	
Goblet Squats	3x10 at RPE 6	20-30 Seconds	
Back Squats	5x5 at 80% / RPE 8 2x10 at 65% / RPE 7	2-3 Minutes 1-2 Minutes	
RDL's	4x8 at RPE 9	1-2 Minutes	
KB Swings	4x20 at RPE 8	1-2 Minutes	
Reverse Hypers	3x20 at RPE 8	30-60 Seconds	

Full Glute Workout 2:

Exercise	Sets/Reps/Time	Rest	Notes
Banded Kneeling Hip Thrusts	3x20 Reps	20-30 Seconds	
Conventional/Sumo Deadlift	5x5 at 80% / RPE 8	2-3 Minutes	
Barbell Hip Thrusts	4x20 at RPE 9	1-2 Minutes	

Sumo Deficit Squat	4x20 at RPE 8	1-2 Minutes	
GHD Back Extensions	3x10 at RPE 8	30-60 Seconds	

Full Glute Workout 3:

Exercise	Sets/Reps/Time	Rest	Notes
Side Lying Hip Abductions	3x20 Reps – Each Side	20-30 Seconds	
Box Squats	5x5 at 80% / RPE 8	2-3 Minutes	
RFESS	3x10 – Each Side at RPE 9	1-2 Minutes	
Single Leg RDL's	3x10 – Each Side at RPE 8	1-2 Minutes	
Single Leg Box Squats	3x5 – Each Side at RPE 7	30-60 Seconds	

Full Glute Workout 4:

Exercise	Sets/Reps/Time	Rest	Notes
Standing Band Kick Backs	3x20 Reps – Each Side	20-30 Seconds	
Back Squats	5x5 at 80% / RPE 8	2-3 Minutes	
Reverse Lunges	3x5 – Each Side at RPE 9	1-2 Minutes	
Step Ups	4x10 at RPE 8	1-2 Minutes	
Crossover Lunges	3x5 – Each Side at RPE 7	30-60 Seconds	

Full Glute Workout 5:

Exercise	Sets/Reps/Time	Rest	Notes
Frog Pumps	3x50 Reps	20-30 Seconds	
Conventional/Sumo Deadlift	5x5 at 80% / RPE 8	2-3 Minutes	
Barbell Hip Thrusts	4x10 at RPE 10	1-2 Minutes	
FFESS	4x10 - Each Side at RPE 8	1-2 Minutes	
Lateral Lunges	3x10 – Each Side at RPE 7	30-60 Seconds	

Metabolid Finisher:

Complete 3-5 rounds of the programmed workout. Take 30-60 seconds rest between sets (1 set = whole workout).

Exercise	Sets/Reps/Time	Rest	Notes
Jump Squats	10-20	0-5 Seconds	
Jump Lunges	10-20	0-5 Seconds	
Wide to Narrow Jump Squats	10-20	0-5 Seconds	
Side Skaters	10-20	0-5 Seconds	

Conclusion

The glutes are a hot topic in any sporting or gym enviroment as they are vital for physical performance, injury prevention and, of course, aesthetics. I am proud to have developed a comprehensive guide on glute training.

Get into the routine of incorporating glute activation and mobility drills into your training regimes and inbetween training sessions if needed. Many of the exercises can be performed in your living room while watching TV, so there's no excuse for getting some extra glute work in.

Remember, building your strength is key to improving any muscle, so use the exercises, programming section, and the free videos to take an educated approach to your programming and training. You'll quickly get the results you want and build an incredible set of glutes.

I hope this book complements your training and benefits your overal physical fitness and physique.

Jay

Glossary of Terms and Equipment

Anatomical Term	Definition/Description
Abdominals Rectus Abdominis / Obliques	Muscles on the front of the abdomen – rectus abdominis (6 pack muscles) / obliques (muscles to the side of the rectus abdominis).
Achilles Tendon	Tendon on the back of the heel.
Adductors	Muscles on the inner side of the thighs.
Calves Gastrocnemius / Soleus	Muscles on the rear of the lower leg.
Core Musculature	The musculature of your torso, but more specifically it is the lumbo-pelvic region (lumbar spine and pelvis, often referred to as your 'lower back'). These muscles are responsible for both stabilisation and the transfer of force from one of movement to the next, for example changing direction.
Deltoid (delts)	Shoulder muscles – anterior delts (front section) / medial delts (middle section) / posterior delts (rear section).
Diaphragm	A dome shaped muscle used in respiration.
Erector Spinae	Muscles that run up either side of the spine
Gluteals (Glutes) Maximus / Medius / Minor	The buttock muscles – major (largest muscle) / medius (middle muscle) / minor (smallest muscle). The gluteal muscles along with the TFL are also referred to as the hip abductors.
Hamstrings Biceps Femoris / Semimembranosus / Semitendinosus	The three muscles on the rear side of the upper leg
Hip Flexors Psoas Major / Iliacus	The muscles on the front of the hips.
Iliotibial Band (ITB)	A band of connective tissue that runs down the outer side of the thigh.
Latissimus Dorsi (Lats)	Mid- back muscle.
Ligaments	A short band of tough, flexible fibrous connective tissue which connects two bones, and helps to hold a joint together.
Muscle Insertion	The insertion is where the muscle ends and is the point at which the muscle is attached to the bone moved by that muscle.
Muscle Origin	The origin is the start of a muscle and is attached to the fixed bone, which is the one which doesn't move during the contraction.
Pectoralis (Pecs) Major / Minor	Chest muscles – major (larger muscle) / minor (smaller muscle)
Peroneals Peroneus Longus / Peroneus Brevis	Muscles on the outer side of the lower legs.
Piriformis	Small muscle underneath the gluteus maximus.
Plantar Fascia	Thick band of connective tissue on the sole of the foot.

Quadratus Lumborum (QL)	Muscles on either side of the lower back.
Quadriceps (Quads) Rectus Femoris / Vastus Medialis / Vastus Intermedius / Vastus Lateralis	The four muscles of the thigh.
Rhomboids	Upper back muscles between the shoulder blades.
Sciatic Nerve	A major nerve extending from the lower end of the spinal cord, through the glutes and down the back of the thigh.
Tendons	A flexible but inelastic cord of strong fibrous collagen tissue attaching a muscle to a bone.
Tensor Fasciae Latae (TFL)	Muscle on the upper outer side of the thigh.
Thoracic Spine	The thoracic spine is the twelve vertebrae between the base of your neck and the bottom of your rib cage. Often when we refer to the thoracic spine in a training environment, we are referring to the muscles which surround it.
Transverse Abdominis (TVA)	The deepest muscle of the abdominal wall and is an integral component of the core
Trapezius (Traps)	Upper back muscle.

Technical Term	Definition/Description
1 Rep Max (1RM)	Most you can lift for 1 rep. I usually work off *Training Maxes*, meaning there is no breakdown in form.
Abduction	Moving limbs back in towards the midline from a lateral position.
Activation	Getting a specific muscle working.
Adduction	Moving a limb laterally away from the midline.
Agonist	The muscle performing the action – the biceps during a biceps curl.
Anatomical Breathing	Synchronizing your breathing with your movements
Antagonist	The muscles that produce an opposing joint torque to the agonist muscles – the triceps during a biceps curl.
Anterior	Front of the body.
Anterior Pelvic Tilt	Pelvis that tilts excessively forward.
Anti-Extension	Resisting forces that try to extend your spine.
Anti-flexion/Lateral Flexion	Resisting forces that try to flex or laterally-flex your spine.
Anti-Rotation	Resisting forces that try to rotate your spine.
Assistance Lifts	Often referred to as *accessory exercises* are also compound movements. They are chosen to develop specific movements or muscle groups that help you to perform the primary lift or specific sporting actions.
Auxiliary Lifts	These single joint exercises. They are chosen to help develop your ability to perform the primary lift or specific sporting actions.
Ballistic	Refers to movements that exhibit maximum acceleration and velocity over short periods of time. Essentially both the concentric (upwards) and eccentric (downwards) phases of this lift are completed with good speed.
Bilateral	Working both sides of the body at the same time.
Biomechanical breathing	Breathing in before or during the eccentric phase, and breathing out during the later stages or after the concentric phase. This method increases total body tension.
Cadence	Stride frequency – the number of strides a runner takes in a minute.
Cervical Spine	Neck – should have a normal lordotic/inwards curve (lordosis).
Compound Exercises/ Movements	Exercises which include multiple joints and muscle groups.
Concentric Phase/Contraction	The upwards phase of a movement, where the muscle(s) are shortening under tension.
Delayed Onset Muscle Soreness (DOMS)	The muscle soreness you feel days after a workout.
Diaphragmatic Breathing	Effectively using the diaphragm during respiration.
Dorsi-Flexion	Refers to flexion at your ankle so that your toes are pointing upwards
Dynamic Effort Method	Lifting at speed – Working between 50-60% of 1RM.
Eccentric Phase/Contraction	The downwards phase of a movement, where the muscle(s) are lengthening under tension.
Extension	when the angle between the two bones increases – straightening a joint.

Fixators & Neutralizers	These muscles help to stabilize the movement.
Flexibility	This refers to a range of motion a muscle can achieve passively, essentially the length it can achieve.
Flexion	When the angle decreases between the two bones attached to either side of the joint being affected – bending a joint.
Foot Strike	The way the foot lands while running.
Golgi Tendon Organ	Receptor organ that senses changes in muscle tension. It can tell muscles to *shut off* when stimulated.
Intra-abdominal Pressure (IAP)	Increased pressure in the abdomen caused by a held breath and contraction of the core muscles.
Isometric Contraction	A muscle contraction where there is no change in muscle length
Lateral-Flexion	Side bending of the spine.
Low Back Pain	Pain, muscle tension, or stiffness localized below the costal margin (bottom rib) and above the inferior gluteal folds (bottom of your buttocks), with or without sciatica.
Lumbar Spine	Lower back – should have a normal lordotic/inwards curve (lordosis).
Lumbo-Pelvic Region	The lumbar spine and pelvis.
Maximal Effort Training	Maximal weight. Working above 90% of your 1RM
Midline	Centre line of the body
Mind-Muscle Connection (MMC)	Consciously thinking about the muscle, you are working to increase its engagement.
Mobility	How freely a joint can move throughout its full range of motion actively. Flexibility is one very important aspect of mobility.
Motor Unit	A neuron and the muscle fibres which it contracts.
Muscle Tension	Tension is often considered to be the same as tightness. However, not only tight or overworked muscles become tense. Muscles that are lengthened or weak can also become tense – examples of these will pop up throughout the book.
Muscle Tightness	This refers to the muscle-length. If a muscle is tight, then it is shortened. Some muscles have the tendency to be shorter and tighter, while others have the tendency to be longer and less activated.
Muscular Imbalance	Occurs when opposing muscles provide different directions of tension due to tightness and/or weakness.
Nasal Breathing	Breathing through the nose.
Negative Stress	Physical Stress that is maladaptive and leads to injuries and regressions in physical performance.
Neutral Pelvis	A pelvis which sits in the optimal position.
Neutral Spine	A spine which is unbent and untwisted, with three natural curves.
Over-Pronation	When your soles turn outwards slightly more than what is considered optimal, placing more load onto the inner side of the ball of your foot.
Plantar-Flexion	Refers to extension at your ankle so that your toes point downwards towards the floor.

Positive Stress	Physical stress that is adaptive and leads to improvements in physical performance.
Posterior	Rear of the body.
Posterior Pelvic Tilt	Pelvis that tilts excessively rearwards.
Posture	A position which aligns your body so that minimal stress is placed on joints and the supporting muscles, tendons, and ligaments. This results in the stresses of daily life being distributed evenly.
Potentiate/Post-Activation Potentiation (PAP)	Potentiation in this context refers to the increase of strength in nerve pathways that have been used previously. Which in layman's terms, means that the associated muscles are primed and working at full capacity. We can use PAP to capitalise on an increase in neuromuscular efficiency – lighter loads often feel abnormally light after working with heavier loads.
Primary Lift	These are compound exercises. They are of most importance in terms of exercise selection as they work movements fully and require the most effort. Therefore, they should be trained first.
Primary/Prime Mover	The muscle most responsible for completing an action.
Pronated Grip	Overhand Grip.
Pronation/Eversion of the Foot	This refers to when the weight it shifted to the inner side of the foot (soles facing outwards).
Proprioception	The body's ability to transmit a sense of position, analyze that information and react to it.
Protraction	Forward movements of structures of the body.
RAMP	A warmup protocol – refers to *Raise, Activate, Mobilise, Potentiate.*
Range of Motion (ROM)	The full movement potential of a joint.
Release Techniques/ Myofascial Release	A method of hands-on therapy that you can perform yourself, usually with a foam roller or massage ball.
Repeated Effort Method	Submaximal weight for maximal reps – I usually program between 60-75% for this method.
Reps & Sets	*Reps* (repetitions) define the number of times you complete an exercise, and *sets* refers to how many times you will repeat that exercise for the specified number of reps. For example, 5 sets of 3 reps (5x3 – sets first), with 2 minute's rest between sets.
Retraction	Rearwards movements of structures of the body.
Sacrum & Coccyx	Back of the pelvis.
Secondary & Tertiary Movers.	Terms used to describe muscles which assist the prime mover (2nd and 3rd to). During compound lifts, often muscles that may not be considered the prime mover, might be producing just as much force to complete the action.
Single-Joint Exercises	Exercises which work a single joint to target a specific muscle.
Strength	Strength is your ability to produce force, the more force you can produce to overcome a resistance (usually tested with a single effort), the stronger you are.
Submaximal Effort Training	Submaximal weight for submaximal reps. Working between 70-90% of 1RM – I usually program between 75-85% of 1RM.
Supinated Grip	Underhand Grip.

Supination/Eversion of the Foot	This refers to when the weight is shifted to the outer side of the foot (soles facing inwards).
Synergists	The muscle(s) which assist the prime mover.
Thoracic Spine	Mid-upper back – should have a normal kyphotic/outwards curve (kyphosis).
Total Body Tension	Creating tension throughout the body by contracting muscles, using the valsalva maneuver and capitalizing on intra-abdominal pressure.
Training Density	The work you can do in each amount of time. For example, 5x10 reps in 15 minutes is less density that 10x10 reps in 15 minutes.
Training Frequency	How often you train.
Training Intensity	How hard you train. For example, how heavy you lift, or how fast you run.
Training Volume	How much you do in a session/workout.
Unilateral	Working one side of the body at a time.
Valsalva Maneuver	A moderately forceful attempted exhalation against a closed airway. Like equalizing your ears on an airplane and blowing against a pinched nose.

Equipment	Definition/Description
Barbell	The barbell is a 7ft long straight bar that weighs 20kg (44lb) and can have weight plates attached to either side. Lower weight bars are available in some gyms.
Dumbbells	Dumbbells are a short bar with a weight (*bell*) at each end. Most gyms will have a wide selection of dumbbells in 1-2.5kg (2-5lb) increments.
Foam Roller	A 90cm foam roller is ideal, (30-45cm rollers are also fine). However, if you choose to spend more you can purchase a 'rumble roller' which allows you to get deeper into specific areas.
Kettlebell	A kettlebell is a large cast-iron ball-shaped weight with a single handle known as the *horn*. Kettlebells usually come in 4kg (9lb) increments.
Massage Ball	You can purchase balls designed specifically for massage, or use a lacrosse ball. Golf balls can be used (rolling the sole of the foot), but they're often too small to be truly effective. Peanut-shaped massage balls allow you to work both sides of your back, while avoiding pressure on your spine.
Plyo Box or Fitness Step	Strength & Conditioning gyms will usually have wooden plyo boxes which allow for three heights to be used (20/24/30 inch), and jerk boxes which stack various box heights. Most commercial gyms will have some form of plyo box, or fitness steps.
Resistance Bands	Long resistance bands come in varying colours, which denote the tension of the band. Yellow: Low tension Red: Medium tension (recommended) Black: Medium tension (greater tension than red)
Small Loop Resistance Bands	Small bands are a great tool for hip and shoulder strengthening drills. The colours of these bands denote varying band tension. However, these colours can vary and therefore, I advise buying a set of 4-5 bands of varying tensions.

Workout Logbook

The following pages are taken from my workout logbook (**http://geni.us/gymlog**) Use them to track your sessions and measure your progress.

Section 1: RAMP Warmup – Complete Prior to Resistance Session

Raise	1.	2.	3.	4.
Activate	1.	2.	3.	4.
Mobilise	1.	2.	3.	4.
Potentiate	1.	2.	3.	4.

Time Taken: __________

Complete Post Resistance Session (Stability & Mobility drills can be practised prior)

Section 2: Conditioning / Metabolic Finisher

Workout/Exercise	Sets/Reps/Time	Rest	Notes - RPE

Time Taken: __________

Section 3: Stability – Neck, Shoulders, Elbows, Wrists, Core/Trunk, Hips, Knees & Ankles

Stability Drills	Sets/Reps/Time	Rest	Notes - RPE

Time Taken: __________

Section 4: Mobility

Release Techniques & Stretches	Sets/Reps/Time	Rest	Notes - RPE

Time Taken: __________

Circle the day: Mon Tue Wed Thu Fri Sat Sun Date: ______

Session Title: ______

Sets	1				2				3				4				5			
Exercise	%	Weight	Reps	RPE	%	Weight	Reps	RPE	%	Weight	Reps	RPE	%	Weight	Reps	RPE	%	Weight	Reps	RPE

Rest Periods: ______ Total Volume: ______ Time Taken: ______

Sets	1				2				3				4				5			
Exercise	%	Weight	Reps	RPE	%	Weight	Reps	RPE	%	Weight	Reps	RPE	%	Weight	Reps	RPE	%	Weight	Reps	RPE

Rest Periods: ______ Total Volume: ______ Time Taken: ______

Sets	1				2				3				4				5			
Exercise	%	Weight	Reps	RPE	%	Weight	Reps	RPE	%	Weight	Reps	RPE	%	Weight	Reps	RPE	%	Weight	Reps	RPE

Rest Periods: ______ Total Volume: ______ Time Taken: ______

Sets	1				2				3				4				5			
Exercise	%	Weight	Reps	RPE	%	Weight	Reps	RPE	%	Weight	Reps	RPE	%	Weight	Reps	RPE	%	Weight	Reps	RPE

Rest Periods: ______ Total Volume: ______ Time Taken: ______

Sets	1				2				3				4				5			
Exercise	%	Weight	Reps	RPE	%	Weight	Reps	RPE	%	Weight	Reps	RPE	%	Weight	Reps	RPE	%	Weight	Reps	RPE

Rest Periods: ______ Total Volume: ______ Time Taken: ______

Section 1: RAMP Warmup – Complete Prior to Resistance Session

Raise	1.	2.	3.	4.
Activate	1.	2.	3.	4.
Mobilise	1.	2.	3.	4.
Potentiate	1.	2.	3.	4.

Time Taken: ________

Complete Post Resistance Session (Stability & Mobility drills can be practised prior)

Section 2: Conditioning / Metabolic Finisher

Workout/Exercise	Sets/Reps/Time	Rest	Notes - RPE

Time Taken: ________

Section 3: Stability – Neck, Shoulders, Elbows, Wrists, Core/Trunk, Hips, Knees & Ankles

Stability Drills	Sets/Reps/Time	Rest	Notes - RPE

Time Taken: ________

Section 4: Mobility

Release Techniques & Stretches	Sets/Reps/Time	Rest	Notes - RPE

Time Taken: ________

Section 5: Resistance Training – Primary, Assistance & Auxiliary Lifts

Circle the day: Mon Tue Wed Thu Fri Sat Sun Date: ______________

Session Title: ________________________

Sets	1				2				3				4				5			
Exercise	%	Weight	Reps	RPE	%	Weight	Reps	RPE	%	Weight	Reps	RPE	%	Weight	Reps	RPE	%	Weight	Reps	RPE

Rest Periods: ______________ **Total Volume:** __________ **Time Taken:** __________

Sets	1				2				3				4				5			
Exercise	%	Weight	Reps	RPE	%	Weight	Reps	RPE	%	Weight	Reps	RPE	%	Weight	Reps	RPE	%	Weight	Reps	RPE

Rest Periods: ______________ **Total Volume:** __________ **Time Taken:** __________

Sets	1				2				3				4				5			
Exercise	%	Weight	Reps	RPE	%	Weight	Reps	RPE	%	Weight	Reps	RPE	%	Weight	Reps	RPE	%	Weight	Reps	RPE

Rest Periods: ______________ **Total Volume:** __________ **Time Taken:** __________

Sets	1				2				3				4				5			
Exercise	%	Weight	Reps	RPE	%	Weight	Reps	RPE	%	Weight	Reps	RPE	%	Weight	Reps	RPE	%	Weight	Reps	RPE

Rest Periods: ______________ **Total Volume:** __________ **Time Taken:** __________

Sets	1				2				3				4				5			
Exercise	%	Weight	Reps	RPE	%	Weight	Reps	RPE	%	Weight	Reps	RPE	%	Weight	Reps	RPE	%	Weight	Reps	RPE

Rest Periods: ______________ **Total Volume:** __________ **Time Taken:** __________

Section 1: RAMP Warmup – Complete Prior to Resistance Session

Raise	**1.**	**2.**	**3.**	**4.**
Activate	**1.**	**2.**	**3.**	**4.**
Mobilise	**1.**	**2.**	**3.**	**4.**
Potentiate	**1.**	**2.**	**3.**	**4.**

Time Taken: ___________

Complete Post Resistance Session (Stability & Mobility drills can be practised prior)

Section 2: Conditioning / Metabolic Finisher

Workout/Exercise	**Sets/Reps/Time**	**Rest**	**Notes - RPE**

Section 3: Stability – Neck, Shoulders, Elbows, Wrists, Core/Trunk, Hips, Knees & Ankles

Time Taken: ___________

Stability Drills	**Sets/Reps/Time**	**Rest**	**Notes - RPE**

Section 4: Mobility

Time Taken: ___________

Release Techniques & Stretches	**Sets/Reps/Time**	**Rest**	**Notes - RPE**

Time Taken: ___________

Circle the day: Mon Tue Wed Thu Fri Sat Sun **Date:** ____________

Session Title: ______________________

Sets	1				2				3				4				5			
Exercise	%	Weight	Reps	RPE	%	Weight	Reps	RPE	%	Weight	Reps	RPE	%	Weight	Reps	RPE	%	Weight	Reps	RPE

Rest Periods: ____________ **Total Volume:** __________ **Time Taken:** _________

Sets	1				2				3				4				5			
Exercise	%	Weight	Reps	RPE	%	Weight	Reps	RPE	%	Weight	Reps	RPE	%	Weight	Reps	RPE	%	Weight	Reps	RPE

Rest Periods: ____________ **Total Volume:** __________ **Time Taken:** _________

Sets	1				2				3				4				5			
Exercise	%	Weight	Reps	RPE	%	Weight	Reps	RPE	%	Weight	Reps	RPE	%	Weight	Reps	RPE	%	Weight	Reps	RPE

Rest Periods: ____________ **Total Volume:** __________ **Time Taken:** _________

Sets	1				2				3				4				5			
Exercise	%	Weight	Reps	RPE	%	Weight	Reps	RPE	%	Weight	Reps	RPE	%	Weight	Reps	RPE	%	Weight	Reps	RPE

Rest Periods: ____________ **Total Volume:** __________ **Time Taken:** _________

Sets	1				2				3				4				5			
Exercise	%	Weight	Reps	RPE	%	Weight	Reps	RPE	%	Weight	Reps	RPE	%	Weight	Reps	RPE	%	Weight	Reps	RPE

Rest Periods: ____________ **Total Volume:** __________ **Time Taken:** _________

Section 1: RAMP Warmup – Complete Prior to Resistance Session

Raise	1.	2.	3.	4.
Activate	1.	2.	3.	4.
Mobilise	1.	2.	3.	4.
Potentiate	1.	2.	3.	4.

Time Taken: __________

Complete Post Resistance Session (Stability & Mobility drills can be practised prior)

Section 2: Conditioning / Metabolic Finisher

Workout/Exercise	Sets/Reps/Time	Rest	Notes - RPE

Time Taken: __________

Section 3: Stability – Neck, Shoulders, Elbows, Wrists, Core/Trunk, Hips, Knees & Ankles

Stability Drills	Sets/Reps/Time	Rest	Notes - RPE

Time Taken: __________

Section 4: Mobility

Release Techniques & Stretches	Sets/Reps/Time	Rest	Notes - RPE

Time Taken: __________

Section 5: Resistance Training – Primary, Assistance & Auxiliary Lifts

Circle the day: Mon Tue Wed Thu Fri Sat Sun Date: ____________

Session Title: ______________________

Sets	1				2				3				4				5			
Exercise	%	Weight	Reps	RPE	%	Weight	Reps	RPE	%	Weight	Reps	RPE	%	Weight	Reps	RPE	%	Weight	Reps	RPE

Rest Periods: ____________ **Total Volume:** __________ **Time Taken:** _________

Sets	1				2				3				4				5			
Exercise	%	Weight	Reps	RPE	%	Weight	Reps	RPE	%	Weight	Reps	RPE	%	Weight	Reps	RPE	%	Weight	Reps	RPE

Rest Periods: ____________ **Total Volume:** __________ **Time Taken:** _________

Sets	1				2				3				4				5			
Exercise	%	Weight	Reps	RPE	%	Weight	Reps	RPE	%	Weight	Reps	RPE	%	Weight	Reps	RPE	%	Weight	Reps	RPE

Rest Periods: ____________ **Total Volume:** __________ **Time Taken:** _________

Sets	1				2				3				4				5			
Exercise	%	Weight	Reps	RPE	%	Weight	Reps	RPE	%	Weight	Reps	RPE	%	Weight	Reps	RPE	%	Weight	Reps	RPE

Rest Periods: ____________ **Total Volume:** __________ **Time Taken:** _________

Sets	1				2				3				4				5			
Exercise	%	Weight	Reps	RPE	%	Weight	Reps	RPE	%	Weight	Reps	RPE	%	Weight	Reps	RPE	%	Weight	Reps	RPE

Rest Periods: ____________ **Total Volume:** __________ **Time Taken:** _________

Section 1: RAMP Warmup – Complete Prior to Resistance Session

Raise	1.	2.	3.	4.
Activate	1.	2.	3.	4.
Mobilise	1.	2.	3.	4.
Potentiate	1.	2.	3.	4.

Time Taken: __________

Complete Post Resistance Session (Stability & Mobility drills can be practised prior)

Section 2: Conditioning / Metabolic Finisher

Workout/Exercise	Sets/Reps/Time	Rest	Notes - RPE

Section 3: Stability – Neck, Shoulders, Elbows, Wrists, Core/Trunk, Hips, Knees & Ankles

Time Taken: __________

Stability Drills	Sets/Reps/Time	Rest	Notes - RPE

Section 4: Mobility

Time Taken: __________

Release Techniques & Stretches	Sets/Reps/Time	Rest	Notes - RPE

Time Taken: __________

Section 5: Resistance Training – Primary, Assistance & Auxiliary Lifts

Circle the day: **Mon Tue Wed Thu Fri Sat Sun Date:** ____________

Session Title: ______________________

Sets	1				2				3				4				5			
Exercise	%	Weight	Reps	RPE	%	Weight	Reps	RPE	%	Weight	Reps	RPE	%	Weight	Reps	RPE	%	Weight	Reps	RPE

Rest Periods: ____________ **Total Volume:** __________ **Time Taken:** _________

Sets	1				2				3				4				5			
Exercise	%	Weight	Reps	RPE	%	Weight	Reps	RPE	%	Weight	Reps	RPE	%	Weight	Reps	RPE	%	Weight	Reps	RPE

Rest Periods: ____________ **Total Volume:** __________ **Time Taken:** _________

Sets	1				2				3				4				5			
Exercise	%	Weight	Reps	RPE	%	Weight	Reps	RPE	%	Weight	Reps	RPE	%	Weight	Reps	RPE	%	Weight	Reps	RPE

Rest Periods: ____________ **Total Volume:** __________ **Time Taken:** _________

Sets	1				2				3				4				5			
Exercise	%	Weight	Reps	RPE	%	Weight	Reps	RPE	%	Weight	Reps	RPE	%	Weight	Reps	RPE	%	Weight	Reps	RPE

Rest Periods: ____________ **Total Volume:** __________ **Time Taken:** _________

Sets	1				2				3				4				5			
Exercise	%	Weight	Reps	RPE	%	Weight	Reps	RPE	%	Weight	Reps	RPE	%	Weight	Reps	RPE	%	Weight	Reps	RPE

Rest Periods: ____________ **Total Volume:** __________ **Time Taken:** _________

Section 1: RAMP Warmup – Complete Prior to Resistance Session

Raise	1.	2.	3.	4.
Activate	1.	2.	3.	4.
Mobilise	1.	2.	3.	4.
Potentiate	1.	2.	3.	4.

Time Taken: __________

Complete Post Resistance Session (Stability & Mobility drills can be practised prior)

Section 2: Conditioning / Metabolic Finisher

Workout/Exercise	Sets/Reps/Time	Rest	Notes - RPE

Section 3: Stability – Neck, Shoulders, Elbows, Wrists, Core/Trunk, Hips, Knees & Ankles

Time Taken: __________

Stability Drills	Sets/Reps/Time	Rest	Notes - RPE

Section 4: Mobility

Time Taken: __________

Release Techniques & Stretches	Sets/Reps/Time	Rest	Notes - RPE

Time Taken: __________

Section 5: Resistance Training – Primary, Assistance & Auxiliary Lifts

Circle the day: Mon Tue Wed Thu Fri Sat Sun **Date:** ____________

Session Title: ______________________

Sets	1				2				3				4				5			
Exercise	%	Weight	Reps	RPE	%	Weight	Reps	RPE	%	Weight	Reps	RPE	%	Weight	Reps	RPE	%	Weight	Reps	RPE

Rest Periods: ____________ **Total Volume:** __________ **Time Taken:** _________

Sets	1				2				3				4				5			
Exercise	%	Weight	Reps	RPE	%	Weight	Reps	RPE	%	Weight	Reps	RPE	%	Weight	Reps	RPE	%	Weight	Reps	RPE

Rest Periods: ____________ **Total Volume:** __________ **Time Taken:** _________

Sets	1				2				3				4				5			
Exercise	%	Weight	Reps	RPE	%	Weight	Reps	RPE	%	Weight	Reps	RPE	%	Weight	Reps	RPE	%	Weight	Reps	RPE

Rest Periods: ____________ **Total Volume:** __________ **Time Taken:** _________

Sets	1				2				3				4				5			
Exercise	%	Weight	Reps	RPE	%	Weight	Reps	RPE	%	Weight	Reps	RPE	%	Weight	Reps	RPE	%	Weight	Reps	RPE

Rest Periods: ____________ **Total Volume:** __________ **Time Taken:** _________

Sets	1				2				3				4				5			
Exercise	%	Weight	Reps	RPE	%	Weight	Reps	RPE	%	Weight	Reps	RPE	%	Weight	Reps	RPE	%	Weight	Reps	RPE

Rest Periods: ____________ **Total Volume:** __________ **Time Taken:** _________

Section 1: RAMP Warmup – Complete Prior to Resistance Session

Raise	1.	2.	3.	4.
Activate	1.	2.	3.	4.
Mobilise	1.	2.	3.	4.
Potentiate	1.	2.	3.	4.

Time Taken: ________

Complete Post Resistance Session (Stability & Mobility drills can be practised prior)

Section 2: Conditioning / Metabolic Finisher

Workout/Exercise	Sets/Reps/Time	Rest	Notes - RPE

Section 3: Stability – Neck, Shoulders, Elbows, Wrists, Core/Trunk, Hips, Knees & Ankles

Time Taken: ________

Stability Drills	Sets/Reps/Time	Rest	Notes - RPE

Section 4: Mobility

Time Taken: ________

Release Techniques & Stretches	Sets/Reps/Time	Rest	Notes - RPE

Time Taken: ________

Section 5: Resistance Training – Primary, Assistance & Auxiliary Lifts

Circle the day: Mon Tue Wed Thu Fri Sat Sun Date: ____________

Session Title: ______________________

Sets	1				2				3				4				5			
Exercise	%	Weight	Reps	RPE	%	Weight	Reps	RPE	%	Weight	Reps	RPE	%	Weight	Reps	RPE	%	Weight	Reps	RPE

Rest Periods: ____________ Total Volume: __________ Time Taken: ________

Sets	1				2				3				4				5			
Exercise	%	Weight	Reps	RPE	%	Weight	Reps	RPE	%	Weight	Reps	RPE	%	Weight	Reps	RPE	%	Weight	Reps	RPE

Rest Periods: ____________ Total Volume: __________ Time Taken: ________

Sets	1				2				3				4				5			
Exercise	%	Weight	Reps	RPE	%	Weight	Reps	RPE	%	Weight	Reps	RPE	%	Weight	Reps	RPE	%	Weight	Reps	RPE

Rest Periods: ____________ Total Volume: __________ Time Taken: ________

Sets	1				2				3				4				5			
Exercise	%	Weight	Reps	RPE	%	Weight	Reps	RPE	%	Weight	Reps	RPE	%	Weight	Reps	RPE	%	Weight	Reps	RPE

Rest Periods: ____________ Total Volume: __________ Time Taken: ________

Sets	1				2				3				4				5			
Exercise	%	Weight	Reps	RPE	%	Weight	Reps	RPE	%	Weight	Reps	RPE	%	Weight	Reps	RPE	%	Weight	Reps	RPE

Rest Periods: ____________ Total Volume: __________ Time Taken: ________

Section 1: RAMP Warmup – Complete Prior to Resistance Session

Raise	1.	2.	3.	4.
Activate	1.	2.	3.	4.
Mobilise	1.	2.	3.	4.
Potentiate	1.	2.	3.	4.

Time Taken: __________

Complete Post Resistance Session (Stability & Mobility drills can be practised prior)

Section 2: Conditioning / Metabolic Finisher

Workout/Exercise	Sets/Reps/Time	Rest	Notes - RPE

Time Taken: __________

Section 3: Stability – Neck, Shoulders, Elbows, Wrists, Core/Trunk, Hips, Knees & Ankles

Stability Drills	Sets/Reps/Time	Rest	Notes - RPE

Time Taken: __________

Section 4: Mobility

Release Techniques & Stretches	Sets/Reps/Time	Rest	Notes - RPE

Time Taken: __________

Section 5: Resistance Training – Primary, Assistance & Auxiliary Lifts

Circle the day: Mon Tue Wed Thu Fri Sat Sun Date: ___________

Session Title: ___________________

Sets	1				2				3				4				5			
Exercise	%	Weight	Reps	RPE	%	Weight	Reps	RPE	%	Weight	Reps	RPE	%	Weight	Reps	RPE	%	Weight	Reps	RPE

Rest Periods: ___________ Total Volume: ________ Time Taken: ________

Sets	1				2				3				4				5			
Exercise	%	Weight	Reps	RPE	%	Weight	Reps	RPE	%	Weight	Reps	RPE	%	Weight	Reps	RPE	%	Weight	Reps	RPE

Rest Periods: ___________ Total Volume: ________ Time Taken: ________

Sets	1				2				3				4				5			
Exercise	%	Weight	Reps	RPE	%	Weight	Reps	RPE	%	Weight	Reps	RPE	%	Weight	Reps	RPE	%	Weight	Reps	RPE

Rest Periods: ___________ Total Volume: ________ Time Taken: ________

Sets	1				2				3				4				5			
Exercise	%	Weight	Reps	RPE	%	Weight	Reps	RPE	%	Weight	Reps	RPE	%	Weight	Reps	RPE	%	Weight	Reps	RPE

Rest Periods: ___________ Total Volume: ________ Time Taken: ________

Sets	1				2				3				4				5			
Exercise	%	Weight	Reps	RPE	%	Weight	Reps	RPE	%	Weight	Reps	RPE	%	Weight	Reps	RPE	%	Weight	Reps	RPE

Rest Periods: ___________ Total Volume: ________ Time Taken: ________

16097615R00053

Printed in Great Britain
by Amazon